Providence

Other volumes in this series:

1   On the Authority of the Bible
2   The Communication of the Gospel in New Testament Times
3   The Miracles and the Resurrection
4   The Authorship and Integrity of the New Testament
5   Authority and the Church
6   Historicity and Chronology in the New Testament
7   Myth and Symbol
8   Christianity in its Social Context
9   Eucharistic Theology Then and Now
10 Word and Sacrament
11 The Scrolls and Christianity

THEOLOGICAL COLLECTIONS

I2

PROVIDENCE

Maurice Wiles (Editor)

Marcus Ward

Geoffrey Parrinder

Norman Goldhawk

Charles Duthie

Huw Owen

Sydney Evans

LONDON

S·P·C·K

1969

First published in 1969
by S.P.C.K.
Holy Trinity Church
Marylebone Road
London N.W.1

Printed in Great Britain by
The Talbot Press (S.P.C.K.)
Saffron Walden, Essex

SBN 281 02340 9

CONTENTS

Notes on Contributors   6

Acknowledgements   7

1. INTRODUCTION
   by Maurice Wiles   9

2. THE BIBLICAL DOCTRINE
   by Marcus Ward   15

3. THE IDEA OF PROVIDENCE IN OTHER RELIGIONS
   by Geoffrey Parrinder   34

4. WILLIAM PALEY: OR THE EIGHTEENTH CENTURY REVISITED
   by Norman Goldhawk   50

5. PROVIDENCE IN THE THEOLOGY OF KARL BARTH
   by Charles Duthie   62

6. PROVIDENCE AND SCIENCE
   by Huw Owen   77

7. TOWARDS A CHRISTIAN DOCTRINE OF PROVIDENCE
   by Sydney Evans   88

NOTES ON CONTRIBUTORS

The Reverend M. F. Wiles is Professor of Christian Doctrine in the University of London, King's College.

The Reverend Dr A. M. Ward is Tutor in New Testament, Richmond College.

The Reverend Dr E. G. Parrinder is Reader in the Comparative Study of Religions in the University of London, King's College.

The Reverend N. P. Goldhawk is Tutor in Church History and the History of Christian Doctrine, Richmond College.

The Reverend Dr C. S. Duthie is Principal of New College, London.

The Reverend H. P. Owen is Reader in the Philosophy of Religion in the University of London, King's College.

The Reverend Canon S. H. Evans is Dean of King's College, London.

ACKNOWLEDGEMENTS

Quotations from the *Revised Standard Version of the Bible*, copyrighted 1946 and 1952 by the Division of Christian Education of the National Council of the Churches of Christ in the United States of America, are used by permission.

Thanks are due to the following for permission to quote from copyright sources:

Clarendon Press: *Essays in Ancient and Modern Philosophy*, by H. W. B. Joseph.

T. & T. Clark: *Church Dogmatics*, by Karl Barth.

Gerald Duckworth & Co Ltd: *The Doctrine of the Atonement*, by J. K. Mozley.

James Nisbet & Co Ltd and Charles Scribner's Sons: *Doctrine of the Creed*, by O. C. Quick.

Oxford University Press: "Ghosts", translated by James Walter McFarlane in *The Oxford Ibsen*, Volume V.

S.C.M. Press Ltd: *Letters and Papers from Prison*, by Dietrich Bonhoeffer.

I

INTRODUCTION

MAURICE WILES

These papers were not designed to provide a comprehensive treatment of the subject of providence. Nor, on the other hand, have they simply been brought together here for the first time from a variety of different sources. The University of London is an entity as liable to the dangers of fragmentation as is the study of theology. It is therefore the custom of the teachers of theology in that university to try to overcome those twin dangers by meeting from time to time for the reading of papers and for discussion among themselves. In the academic year 1967-8, six such meetings were held, all concerned with the theme of providence. To that degree there was an overall unity of design. But the particular topics for each occasion were chosen not so much to ensure that all aspects of the subject were covered as to give an opportunity for different scholars to introduce discussion on the general theme from the standpoint of their own special interest. The papers printed here were originally written for that purpose alone without any view to publication, but are now being given a wider circulation after their authors have had the opportunity of revising them in the light both of the series of papers as a whole and of the discussion which followed the delivery of each.

Providence is not a subject which stands at the centre of much contemporary theological debate, yet it can never be very far away from the centre of religious concern. "To deny providence", wrote H. H. Farmer, "*is* to deny religion."[1] These papers, therefore, should not be seen as seeking to provide answers to questions that are already being widely discussed, but rather as a reminder of certain important questions that must not be shirked together with some suggestions of the ways in which they may most fruitfully be raised.

[1] *The World and God* (1935), p. 99.

The first two papers go a long way to substantiate the truth of Farmer's dictum about the coincidence of the spheres of providence and religion. In the first paper Dr Marcus Ward gives a sensitive and probing survey of biblical attitudes. Difficulties inherent in the idea of providence were clearly felt and honestly discussed. Yet it is not the quality or the conclusions of that discussion that emerge as the characteristic contribution of the biblical writings. As Dr Ward puts it, "the *arguments* for providence are less strong than the faith in it". The concept of providence stands out from his study as something that for biblical faith is both essentially religious and religiously essential.

This approach to the matter is reinforced by Dr Geoffrey Parrinder's examination of the very different material provided by Islam, by Hindu Theism, and by Buddhism. In each case he shows how something closely akin to a belief in providence keeps breaking through, even where the logical structure of the religion seems to militate strongly against any such belief. In Islam, the most strongly theistic of the three, Allāh might sometimes seem too transcendent a deity for the concept of providence to flourish; but Allāh is also the Compassionate Compassionator. In Hinduism the doctrine of *Karma* might seem to exclude any understanding of providence, yet the Gītā points in a very different direction. Even in so-called atheistic Buddhism, the Buddha can come to be regarded as "Father of the World, the Refuge, Healer, and Protector of all creatures". Even in the apparently most unpromising soil, a religious faith in providence will be found to grow.

Thus the concept is one of importance not only to Christianity but to other religions as well. But there is a distinctively Christian view of providence and Dr Ward is undoubtedly right in claiming that, whether or not the fact has always been adequately emphasized, it is belief in the cross and resurrection of Christ which ought to provide the distinctively Christian understanding of the matter.

The next two papers consider the teaching of two thinkers from the course of Christian history. It would be difficult to find two Christian writers whose approach to Christian faith was more diametrically opposed than William Paley and Karl Barth—Paley the most famous (or, in the judgement of some, infamous) and extreme exponent of natural theology and the argument from design; Karl Barth the most vigorous and implacable opponent of any such approach to theology. Yet for both providence is a central issue. Natural religion and biblical religion may not always understand providence in the same way; but it is equally close to the centre of religion for both. For Paley divine providence is to be seen in a whole host of examples of God's beneficent design clearly present in the basic ordering of the natural world, for Barth that providence can only be seen in and through God's self-revelation in the person of Jesus Christ; it is the fact of that revelation—and that alone—which opens up the possibility for any Christian doctrine of providence.

Both Mr Goldhawk and Dr Duthie have that fundamental sympathy with the approach of the one whose thought they are setting out to expound together with a readiness to pass critical judgement which are the essential ingredients in all work of interpretation. It is interesting to notice how in each case their most fundamental criticism points in the same direction. We cannot, Mr Goldhawk argues, accept that the order of events as they occur is providential in the way that Paley did; but may we not, he suggests, be able to express the truth after which Paley was striving by claiming that the world is of such a nature that man can turn to good whatever circumstance may confront him? In other words, more place must be given to man's role in any talk about providence that is to carry conviction. So too Dr Duthie, while showing how Barth gives full verbal assent to the real freedom of human actions in the world, finds himself bound to question how deep that assent goes, how effectively it is integrated into the fundamental structure and drive of Barth's thought. "In his endeavour to do justice to the Lordship of God", writes Dr Duthie, "does he do less than justice to human freedom and activity?" Thus from the very different angle of a study of Barth's teaching the same issue forces itself on our attention as arises from the study of Paley—the relation of our talk of providence to our understanding of human freedom and human responsibility.

Both Paley and Barth belong to that later strand of Christian history which has had to take account of the rise of modern science and modern scientific method. Yet for very different reasons (in Paley's case of date, in Barth's case of fundamental theological method) neither can be said to have taken full account of the changes in human thought and human sensibility which characterize the world of today.

In the paper that follows Mr H. P. Owen examines the ways in which the idea of providence and the study of the natural sciences impinge on one another. He avoids the very general approach which characterizes much popular discussion of religion and science and breaks the question down into the various specific points at which some interaction might properly be claimed. His method is particularly valuable in the light of assertions frequently to be heard, claiming either total conflict and incompatibility on the one hand or total unrelatedness and divorce of spheres of interest on the other.

He finds some aspects of a belief in providence which are only affected minimally, if at all, by the natural sciences but other aspects for which the relationship with scientific knowledge is of great significance. As the outcome of his investigation Mr Owen is bold enough to "conclude that science confirms belief in God as a controlling Mind that sets the physical stage for the human drama"

Two further sentences follow that one, to form the close of Mr Owen's paper. "But concerning the drama itself and any specific divine intervention in it science has nothing to say. Hence I can bring you only to the threshold of *Geschichte* and, *a fortiori, Heilsgeschichte*." At this point, perhaps more than at any other, the selectiveness of these studies on providence becomes apparent. For there is no historian or philosopher of history to carry on across that threshold the torch which Mr Owen has brought so far.

Dr Duthie describes in the course of his paper the way in which Karl Barth speaks of signs of God's rule in history. Barth is careful to insist that these signs are only to be detected from within the experience of God's self-revelation in Jesus Christ. Others in the past have more incautiously claimed those same historical phenomena as direct evidence of God's providential rule. Such a handling of historical evidence is very similar to the attitude of Paley to the evidence of the natural world—indeed Paley himself uses historical evidence in just this kind of way in his discussion of the rapid rise and spread of early Christianity.[2] From the vantage point of hindsight, such an approach tends to concentrate its gaze too exclusively on those happenings which support its case.

If we reject, as we must, such exaggerated and oversimplified assertions, we ought not to be led on to speak instead of a complete divorce between history and theology any more than we should do so in the case of the relationship between natural science and theology. Providence is not a term that either can or should belong to the vocabulary or conceptual scheme of the historian in his historical work. Yet the philosopher of history is concerned in his own way with problems not unrelated to those which the theologian is seeking to explicate when he speaks of a divine providence in history. The historian aims not merely to construct a narrative of the past but a *significant* narrative; he is concerned to tell a story that has some sort of shape or meaning.[3] It is interesting to find Professor Gallie speaking of a partial analogy between the unity to be found in successful works of history and that which characterizes the story that runs from Abraham through Isaac and Jacob to

[2] *Evidences of Christianity*, Ch. 9.
[3] Cf. W. H. Walsh, *"Meaning" in History* in P. Gardiner, *Theories of History* (1960), pp. 296-307; W. B. Gallie, *Philosophy and the Historical Understanding* (1964), Chs. 2 and 3.

Joseph—for, as both Dr Ward and Canon Evans point out, the Joseph saga is perhaps the most outstanding example of the biblical conception of providence. Certainly the pitfalls involved in any Christian talk of providence in relation to the historical process as a whole are numerous; but that is not to say that they are inescapable. The theologian needs to listen attentively not only to the historian himself and to the detailed findings of his studies, but also to those who reflect philosophically on the implications of the way in which the historian sets about his task.

Here undoubtedly is a most important aspect of the subject which is not included in the papers given here. What the final paper seeks to do is to take account in a general way of that contemporary awareness of the world of which modern scientific and historical study are both causes and particular symptoms and to ask what—in such a setting—a Christian doctrine of providence might look like, to ask indeed whether—in such a setting—a Christian doctrine of providence is possible at all. What strikes me most forcefully about Canon Evans' paper is how, for all the evident modernity of his approach and his profound sensitivity to the outlook of the present age, both the really pressing perplexities and the lines of positive affirmation remain remarkably close to those that emerged from the initial study of the biblical approach. The central problem is not new; it is the age-old problem of evil, whose urgency and poignancy must never be played down just because it is old and familiar. Dr Ward, as we have seen, contrasts the strength of faith in providence with the comparative weakness of arguments for it in the Bible. So too for Canon Evans "providence" is indicative of "a faith to live by", yet he remains very uncertain about the possibility of giving expression to any "Christian doctrine of providence". Moreover, the central factor in establishing and maintaining such a faith in face of the horrors of evil and of suffering is still the cross of Jesus.

If the conception of a faith in providence but no doctrine of providence were to imply that that faith should be exempted from the challenging questionings of the critical intelligence, it would soon degenerate into superstition. It is perfectly obvious that Canon Evans means no such thing; his paper is automatic refutation of any such suggestion, since it is itself an example of precisely such questioning. Doubt about the feasibility of a Christian doctrine of providence can be understood in two other ways. It might mean that, though we hold such a faith and believe that we hold it rationally, we are so aware of the problematic character of any form of statement in which we seek to give that faith expression that we would prefer not to speak of it as a "doctrine"—with all the overtones that that word carries of a comparatively firm, clear-cut, and adequate expression of a truth. It might also mean that—to use Canon Evans' phrase—the "model" of providence has in the past been used to co-ordinate too many disparate elements in the experience of faith and that it has thereby given rise to more confusion than illumination. After all, if "to deny providence *is* to deny religion", it is clearly a concept of extreme generality and it may well be that the varied concerns which have traditionally been expressed in terms of a doctrine of providence can more satisfactorily be expressed in a number of other ways.

But, however that may be, the concerns are real. They are central to religion and they are open to challenge. The theologian must not neglect them. These papers are offered in the hope that they may suggest some of the lines along which a discussion of them can most usefully be carried on.

2

THE BIBLICAL DOCTRINE

MARCUS WARD

'There's a special providence in the fall of a sparrow"—this, one of the two quotations on the theme which every schoolboy knows, brings us to the heart of the matter. Even the sparrow, rated by Matthew 10. 29ff at two a penny or, more subtly, by Luke 12. 6 at five for tuppence, the odd one thrown in for luck, does not fall "without your Father". *Without?* There is a wide field of possibility. Without his providing, preparing, arranging, managing, governing, guiding; without his foresight, anticipation, direction, control? The versions adding βουλή to Matthew would have it "without his will", and the Lucan "forgotten in God's sight", "without his knowledge".

Providence is a word with a long history, often darkened by narrow and untrue conceptions of its meaning. Admittedly the narrow and untrue conceptions of its meaning. Admittedly the word πρόνοια, literally foresight, common enough in Greek philosophy, is not biblical, but the idea is and the single use in Wisdom 14. 2f

> Wisdom was the craftsman that built [the ship]
> and your providence, Father, is what pilots it

suggests the connotation: that he who created the world remains in control of all that he has made, providing for future needs. All in all, we have a general concept of the prescient and beneficent care and rule of the heavenly Father "whose never-failing providence ordereth all things both in heaven and earth".

At first sight and on the simple view the teaching of the Bible seems quite clear. For example:

> He who dwells in the shelter of the Most High,
>   who abides in the shadow of the Almighty,
> will say to the Lord, "My refuge and my fortress;
>   my God, in whom I trust." . . .
> A thousand may fall at your side,
>   ten thousand at your right hand;

> but it will not come near you.
> You will only look with your eyes
>   and see the recompense of the wicked. (Ps. 91. 1, 2, 7, 8)

Here is unambiguous certainty that the good will be preserved
through any evil and will be spared that which befalls others
especially the ungodly whose reward is evil. The same understanding of, and confidence in, the providential care of God can be read
in such psalms as Psalm 27 or 121 and in the dominical word with
reference to which this paper began. Here the ground of faith and
assurance is a fundamental conviction in the sovereign purpose
and power of God. Many are (or, perhaps, have been) content to rest
upon the words of the Bible, such as those that have been quoted.
For most, however, such simple trust is inhibited by deep and
urgent questions which demand an answer before there can be
confident assurance as to the beneficent ordering, preservation, and
government of the world by God. How precisely may God be said to
act in the world? In face of the persistence of evil can we believe
that it will not triumph? Are we at the mercy of God or of malig-
nant forces? These, and other questions which will emerge, compel
us to look more closely at the grounds on which the psalmist
bases his belief and Jesus his assurance. It is the purpose of this
paper to demonstrate that the understanding of providence is the
consequence of the immediate experience of God; a religious experience in which prayer on the one side is met on the other by
an answering reality which transforms prayer into assurance. Of
this experience of man's dependence on God and God's gracious
dealings with man the Bible is the story.

Amid the mass of evidence, often conflicting and sometimes
contradictory, it is not easy to pick our way. We have fallen back
on a simple expedient. In 1935 the General Assembly of the Church
of Scotland commended a *Short Statement of the Church's Faith*.
It contains a summary definition of our theme suggesting general
headings under which we may usefully survey the biblical evidence:

> In his infinite wisdom, God governs all things and overrules all events,
> for perfectly wise and loving ends. He has every human life in his
> gracious and holy keeping.

1. *God Governs All Things*

The Bible begins with the creation of the world in orderly sequence
and ends with the expectation of the return of the Lord Jesus to
bring history to a close. Genesis 1—2 supported by constant references in the Psalter and by Paul in such a passage as Romans 8,

declares that God alone is creator and sustainer. He appears on the scene, without definition or description of his being or character, already active—and that in itself represents a profound theological judgement. He does not then remove himself from the scene, but continues his work of creation in preserving what he has made. He gives or withdraws life as he wills and man's life is wholly dependent upon him. If some respond and some reject, none is beyond his knowledge or outside his care. Without God man is as grass. God gives food to man and beast. He rules all the forces of nature which is seen to serve his purposes, to reveal his power and wisdom, to show his goodness and glory. That there is regular working of natural forces is accepted, but on the understanding that apart from the will of God there is no order. Whatever he wills he does and nothing is too wonderful for him to do. Thus "miracles" are taken for granted as due to immediate divine initiative. God's character can best be read in his continuous dealings with the world he has made. It is not at the mercy of fate or of chance.

While the biblical doctrine of creation, thus broadly outlined, stresses that man is the culmination, the clear-cut distinction between man and the rest of creation, involving the view that nature is man's servant and for his use, was less prominent in earlier days when man was seen to be very much a part of nature. Thus for prophet and psalmist divine dominion and control were not limited to man. Nature as a whole was subject to God and the object of his care. The belief that "the Lord is good to all, and his compassion is over all that he has made" (Ps. 145. 9) is illustrated in Job 38—39 where the divine provision extends from inanimate nature to the whole range of the animal kingdom. Again, he who is to make a new Covenant with Israel and Judah is the same Lord of hosts "who gives the sun for light by day and the fixed order of the moon and the stars for light by night, who stirs up the sea so that its waves roar" (Jer. 31. 35). "If this fixed order departs from before me," the oracle goes on, "then shall the descendants of Israel cease from being a nation before me for ever" (Jer. 31. 36).

In such ways the Old Testament sees human destiny to be closely related to the rest of creation. Animals, even the earth itself, are involved in the pains and joy of men. "Cursed is the ground because of you", says God to fallen Adam (Gen. 3. 17). On account of the wickedness of men "He turns rivers into a desert, springs of water into thirsty ground, a fruitful land into a salty waste" (Ps. 107. 33f). On the other hand, when the Lord does a new thing for Israel, even the meanest creatures are to have a share in the benefits (Isa. 43. 14-21). In the New Testament also there is the expectation that all nature will share in the general restoration. It is the *whole* creation which "waits with eager longing for the revealing of the sons of God" (Rom. 8. 18ff)—that culmination of the process of creation in the manifestation of free beings united in the family of God which undergirds the certainty that God continues to govern all that he has made.

Nor may we forget that part of the larger messianic hope, in both Testaments and in the intertestamental writings, was the new heaven and the new earth (Isa. 65. 17; Enoch 45. 4f; Rev. 21. 1).

2. *God Overrules All Events*

The very small portion of the evidence adduced above makes it clear that the world of nature has something to say about the meaning of God's "long-term planning" as providence has been neatly termed. Paul speaking at Lystra (Acts 14. 15ff) and at Athens (Acts 17. 24ff) and writing to the Roman Church (Rom. 1. 18ff) makes the point that God intends men thus to learn something of his mind, character, and ways. The best and clearest evidence, however, is found in his dealings with persons, in terms of events rather than of things. The Christian missionary knows how the biblical concept of history as having meaning and goal comes as something new and liberating to those who have regarded the time process as never-ending repetition, leading nowhere. In the first preaching of the gospel to the Gentiles it was this conviction that gave force to the message. Yet, if the revelation in Christ was thus to give new awareness of the meaning of providence as disclosed in God's dealings with men, the point had been taken long before.

Dr O. C. Quick has argued that "the most obviously distinctive characteristic of Hebrew theology is its belief in God's guidance of history. We owe the familiar idea of providence to the religious legacy we have received from Israel".[1] This must be taken with caution. On the one hand, the idea of divine intervention in, and control of, history is not unique to Israel; nor was it, on the other hand, in view of the tensions of experience, quite as simple as is often suggested. Nevertheless, one of the clearest and most effective differences between Hebrew religion, as we see it in the Old Testament, and that of Greece and Rome lies in the Hebrew emphasis on that divine activity in history which enables men to come to a knowledge of God. It is true that we read in classical literature many stories of the active intervention of the gods in human affairs; but they are fundamentally unlike the Old Testament accounts of God's dealings with Israel, and beyond. There are reasons for this. On the one hand, there is, in classical mythology,

[1] *Doctrines of the Creed* (1938), p. 69.

no idea that in what the gods do they have the purpose of bringing to men the truth about themselves and their divine nature. And, on the other hand, the possibility of such knowledge is excluded by the very lack of unity in action which the gods reveal. Each divine being can reveal only himself; and they reveal themselves as contrasting with one another, not as manifesting complementary aspects of the one divine nature. Polytheism, as has been said, bars the way to revelation.

Again Quick seems right when he emphasizes "the difference between the catastrophic view of history which we find in the Bible, and the evolutionary view which was the discovery of nineteenth-century humanism".

> But [he goes on] the two views have at least this much in common, that both interpret history as a series of caused and causative happenings which led up to a great denouement in which the significance of all is seen. To the Jew, Jehovah was essentially the living God who acted in history and controlled the issues of events. In his religious philosophy history itself is the story of God's mighty acts, wherein God achieves his purposes for the vindication of his chosen and the punishment of those who disobey him.[2]

Regarded objectively, history for the Israelite might appear disastrous rather than "providential" in the easy and conventional sense. It posed continual tension between the poles of a protecting covenant God and of a judging God.[3] Nevertheless, the prophets claimed to be able to read its meaning in the light of their belief that Yahweh was the God of all the world. "It is God, supreme and almighty, who interprets, predicts and controls his people's history, and not their history, which, in its gradual evolution, is to make God's soverignty and omnipotence manifest to that experience."[4] It is God who brought Israel from Egypt and the Philistines from Crete, in whose hands the empires are but instruments, who brings in new epochs, raising leaders and guiding events. History, indeed, has evidence of its own. When the writers interpret the story of their nation as illustrating the ruinous consequences of disobedience, they are drawing on plain facts. The same can be said of the judgements on empires which, in their pride, forget the precarious nature of historic achievement and overestimate their security. But, if and when better times come, the prophets do not regard this as evidence that *now* God is remembering his people. It is because they believe that God comes into history that they are confident that he will not forsake them.

[2] Ibid., p. 69.
[3] For this, and other points, I am indebted to Professor P. R. Ackroyd.
[4] G. A. Smith, *Isaiah* (1927), Vol. II, p. 24.

The biblical view of God as looking ahead and guiding events in the life of Israel has its great illustration in the story of the Exodus. The relationship here of event and faith is so complex as to make it doubtful whether there is any value in the mere reference without a discussion necessarily fuller than is possible here. Whatever were the precise happenings; however we seek to disentangle the psychical and the physical; whether or not there was a special "providence" at work, the men of Israel believed thereafter: "Thou didst blow with thy wind, the sea covered them; they sank as lead in the mighty waters" (Exod. 15. 10) and gloried in the whole train of mighty and redeeming action. The very richness of the tradition both conceals the precise events and illumines the impact of their interpretation in the light of the belief in Yahweh as one fully in control of the situation. The event itself may be little apart from the prophetic interpretation. However that may be, there emerged a *religious* fact which can be said to have changed the course of history. The centrality of the Exodus for the religious faith of Israel is such as to provide the focal point for the interpretation of biblical theology, not least for that aspect now under consideration.

The Joseph saga, told without any visible divine intervention or new revelation, provides the outstanding example of how God's dealing with an individual life can be seen, to a certain type of understanding, to be bound up with the larger purpose. A "wisdom" narrative, it tells how divine providence thwarts the evil designs of men and turns their malice to profit in bringing a man to his life-work for the salvation of his people. "The evil you planned to do to me", concludes Joseph to his brothers, "has by God's design been turned to good, that he might bring about, as indeed he has, the deliverance of a numerous people" (Gen. 50. 20). Behind this lay a complex series of events too familiar to need recapitulation here. Are they to be regarded as casual or causal? The distinction is not always easy to draw when trying to interpret history. There seems good reason to reject the view that God directly and deliberately causes each separate event. The biblical understanding of providence never means that. It allows for human freedom and for the evil which God may permit but does not directly will. Yet when Joseph saw the events as lying within the overarching wisdom and power of God, he was but reflecting a faith in divine providence which overrules the stubbornness of nature and the perversity of men with a view, in this case, to the making of a chosen people.

We have already noted an element wherein the Old Testament stands over against the thought of Greece and Rome. Another *differentia* is the stress in the Hebrew tradition on the distinction of God from man and hence on the knowledge of God made possible by active divine self-relevation. Thus the characteristic note is testimony, with its distinctive "Thus saith the Lord", rather than speculation. We hear through the Bible the voice of witness to one who has revealed himself in the history of his people, and even beyond. His words and his law, his mercy and his judgements are the evidence of revelation. Therefore those who say: "The Lord will not do good nor will he do ill" (Zeph. 1. 12) are rightly condemned. The idea of God as the king who had ceased to exercise his authority is intolerable just because the reality of revelation is taken seriously. It may be that the witness was more effective as evidence of divine revelation when the miracles of the Old Testament were accepted as they stood without any doubts as to their historical character. But we do well to remember that much of such detail in the narratives, both those cited above and others, belongs to but does not simply constitute the series of unambiguously historical events to which the prophets appealed for the vindication of their witness. The appeal was not to the extraordinary in the natural order but to the activity of God. In this respect they were certain that God enabled them to prophesy truly. Their witness was one of interpretation.

It could be argued that the biblical way of regarding the world as the sphere wherein God can act at any time is truer to the facts than the negative assumption that he never acts at all. Yet we may well ask whether the actual course of events does, in fact, justify the prophets' claim, based on what they had come to know and experience of the character of God, that he cares for men and guides the events that touch them.

History, indeed, is the record not only of God's ordering but of man's rebellion. It bears, as we have noted, the signs of his judgement as well as of his protection. There is the weight of negative evidence for providence. It is just because God is in control of history that kingdoms fall in their pride and the evil schemes of men come to nothing. There have been many who have learned through the discipline of events what Daniel taught Nebuchadnezzar: "Your kingdom shall be sure for you from the time that you know that Heaven rules" (Dan. 4. 26). There is point in Berdyaev's argument that Daniel's interpretation of Nebuchadnezzar's dream is the first example of the attribution of design to history.[5]

We have already made use of the creation story in Genesis. We do not forget that it goes on to make clear that man, the present culmination of creation on earth, has fallen from his high estate.

[5] *The Meaning of History* (1936), p. 29.

What he has become is not what God meant him to be. The world and all in it belongs to God. In itself it is good and the home of his children. But they, made free to obey or to rebel, have chosen darkness rather than light. This "Fall" has infected the whole race with frustration. For this reason the creative process is not yet complete, as Paul makes clear (Rom. 8. 18ff). The goal is, as we have said, the manifestation of free beings united in the family of God. He alone can bring good out of evil. Hence his "long-term planning" must include the restoration of man into fellowship. This, foreshadowed in the Old Testament, becomes fully revealed in Christ in whom God has accomplished the new creative event (2 Cor. 5. 17). The divine guidance of events from creation, through the history of Israel, comes to its climax in the incarnation (Matt 21. 33ff).

That Jesus was born in the fullness of time (Gal. 4. 4) is usually interpreted to include the thought that, under divine providence, a preparatory work had been done, previous history pointing forward to the great event. This being so, if we discern the hand of God in the working of nature and the common ways of life, we see it most strikingly in the great crises of history, and especially in the coming down of God's Son to share our life. The daily round may give assurance of the divine care and purpose ever at work; but the crisis reveals the method. To make the point clear we must anticipate a theme later to be developed—the centrality of the cross in our thinking about providence. Here in one historic event we see the wickedness of men in opposition to the Son of God and rejecting him; the exposure of human sinfulness and the divine judgement on it; and the way in which, *in the providence of God* the very instrument of sin becomes the means of redemption. Men were free to put Jesus to death in order to bring his work to an end. God did not intervene to prevent the crucifixion nor did Jesus summon the legions of angels to his help. Yet by his passion he became Lord and Saviour (Phil. 2. 8-11). The sin of men and the purpose of God are both ineluctable facts, and God uses the sin to serve the purpose—the supreme example of that overruling of all events of which we have considered some of the evidence.

3. *For Perfectly Wise and Loving Ends*

From the great example and proof of the divine overruling we pass to consider the purpose—"for perfectly wise and loving ends". Broadly speaking the biblical evidence suggests as the immediate concern of providence the fulfilment of God's purpose for the salvation of his people. At the time of God's choosing it seemed a very trivial matter—a people without land or history; as yet without the rudiments of civilization; desert tribes at the mercy of their neighbours; child and slave indeed as Hosea insisted (Hos. 11. 1ff). We can appreciate that the very wonder of being chosen as a peculiar people made it difficult for the Hebrews to understand that the choice was not on their merits or for their sole advantage. It was no small thing that the prophets came to see that there was divine concern for the Gentiles also and to recognize the action and purpose of Yahweh in the history of other nations (Isa. 2. 2ff; 19. 23ff). That he is in control of all the nations, first explicit in Amos (Amos 9. 7), runs through to Paul (Rom. 9. 14ff). He made them all and they all owe him obedience. At times he seems to move them about as on a chess board, plucking up and destroying or repenting of the evil intended (Jer. 18. 7ff). The Psalms speak of him educating and reproving the nations as well as Israel (Ps. 46. 10; 65. 2ff; 94. 10f) until they all join in the outburst of praise rising from all his creatures (Ps. 150).

The later prophets may seem to lay stress less on history than on the apocalypse of divine intervention. Yet there is a sense in which this is in fact the appeal to history on the widest scale. It is in apocalypse that we find the first full understanding of the unity of history in its cosmological, human, and spiritual aspects. This is clearly to be seen in the book of Daniel, where the gulf between the kingdom of God and the human empire has grown so wide as to require divine intervention to restore the rule of God. Written against the background of disaster about to overwhelm the chosen people and their faith, the book illustrates the fact that the man of God is most inclined to look for meaning in history in times of catastrophe.

The philosophy of history, embryonic in Daniel, was worked out by Paul in the light of fuller experience of God's dealing with men. In Rom. 5. 12ff and 9—11, he outlines stages in the education of mankind: the Adam era of innocence; the Moses era of training under the law; the Christ era of grace. In it all the divine purposes of mercy and justice are seen to work out by a process of selection, and then Paul reaches the daring conclusion that Judaism was merely a parenthesis in history. This outline is further developed in Ephesians with its wide vistas of the divine purpose for man and the world built on the great premiss that with the coming of Christ, in whom it is God's purpose to sum up all, there is a new start in history, the old divisions done away and the unity of mankind restored (Eph. 1. 10; 2. 14ff; 3. 1ff; 4. 24).

This makes explicit that which is implicit through the New Testament. The coming of Christ represents not merely the end of

one epoch of history, the completion of a significant stage in the
carrying out of God's purpose for his world, but also the beginning
of another chapter in the history of man, in which the Church now
has the central place, which will reveal to the universe the meaning
of that purpose—till he come.

Thus through the Bible, from creation to the coming Day of the
Lord, runs a divine purpose, wise and loving, giving unity and
meaning to the course of events and the vicissitudes of history. In
the whole process man, made in the image of God, is seen to be held
in special regard by his Maker despite his failure to rise to his high
calling. One evidence of this is the way in which God allows
and uses the co-operation of men in the working out of his
purposes. His chosen instruments come not only from his people
but also from the nations (Isa. 10. 5ff). He knows them before they
need to be used (Isa. 41. 2f; Jer. 1. 5; Gal. 1. 15) and may constrain
them to serve against their inclination (Jer. 20. 7) or, as in the case
of Pharoah, to their immediate disadvantage. He may even use
lawless men whose evil deeds unconsciously serve his purpose
(Acts 2. 23).

The sense of God's concern with human affairs is one element
in the biblical tradition which checked despondency and kindled
hope. It also rebuked pride and encouraged humility. This characteristic of Old Testament piety at its best seems so important to our
theme as to call for a detailed illustration.

There is a significant view of man given by Sophocles in the
famous chorus from the *Antigone* (lines 332ff):

> Many things there are, weird and wonderful,
> None more so than man.
> He sails beyond the seas, lashed white by winter wind,
> Piercing the waters roaring round.
> He furrows the unwithered earth, greatest of immortal divinities,
> Year by year with horse and plough he turns the sod.
> Winged birds he snares, wild beasts and fish;
> Wild horse, untamed mountain bull, he tames and yokes.
> He has taught himself speech also, and wisdom,
> And customs of law whereby men live in communities . . .
> In all things he finds him a way.
> Death is too great for him, yet he devises healing of sickness.
> He has art and skill to invent . . .

Compare this psalm of man with the view given in Psalm 8. How
striking is the contrast between the reiterated *he, he, he* of the
Greek poem and the adoring *Thou, Thou, Thou* of the Hebrew.
Both recognize man to be the crown of creation; but while the
one attributes man's authority over nature to his own strength and

wisdom, the other accepts it as the gift of God. In the biblical view man is what he is, and does what he does, in virtue of divine creation. The whole is coloured by the sense of creatureliness and adoration.

4. *God has Every Human Life in his Gracious and Holy Keeping*

The argument thus far has tended to relate the idea of providential oversight and control to mankind at large. What of its exercise in regard to the individual for whom the problems of the meaning and purpose of his own life may be even more urgent than those of the universe? That God "has every human life in his gracious and holy keeping" may not be readily apparent, especially in the Old Testament where the individual seems to matter only *qua* member of the community whose fortunes are the important thing and with which those of the individual are bound up.

It is true that in old Israel the law recognized individual as well as corporate responsibility so that the distinction must not be overdrawn. Yet the value and responsibility of the individual has a recognition in the later prophets not so prominent earlier, well illustrated by Jeremiah's stress on the appropriation by each member of the Covenant made with Israel (Jer. 31. 34). Granted that in this respect we can trace some development of thought, why did it take so long to relate the idea of providence to *each* man? It has been suggested that there is an element in the older biblical tradition not unlike the later Moslem doctrine that to take note of individuals is beneath the dignity of God who concerns himself only with the universal order. It is more likely that the limitation runs *pari passu* with the lack of concern for the concept of the immortality of the individual man which is part of the complex understanding of the corporate nature of human life. Early vague hints of some kind of survival mean little. God does not appear to take interest in the departed. The faithful of Psalm 39. 12f is a passing guest who departs and is no more. God is his temporary host. With him a man sojourns for a while and then moves on beyond his jurisdiction. So Psalm 6. 5:

> In death there is no remembrance of thee;
> in Sheol who can give thee praise?

It is the destiny and continuation of the people that has significance rather than that of the individual member.

We may not, and do not, conclude that there can be no valid concept of providence without belief in life after death. What we have already seen of the Old Testament understanding of community in relation to the living God excludes that. We do contend that the real importance of the individual, and so the personal reference of providence, is bound up with the development of the doctrine of the life to come. It is consequently in the New Testament that providence takes full cognizance of the individual as in the dominical word of Matthew 10. 28ff; Luke 12. 4ff. To this may be added the promise that the Holy Spirit will abide with men to be guide and teacher (John 14—16) and its fulfilment in the frequent intervention by the Holy Spirit in the lives of individuals (Acts 8. 29; 10. 19; 16. 7, etc.). The same emphasis can be traced in our Lord's teaching on prayer, and his frequent "How much more"; in the insistence that God made man in his image in order to have beings able to respond to him in love and to offer true worship (e.g. Acts 17. 27f; John 4. 23); and in Paul's accounts of the divine dealings with man from foreknowledge to glory (Rom. 8. 28ff; Eph. 1. 4ff). It is not, we repeat, new doctrine but a closer application to the individual in contrast to the earlier concern with God's dealings with his people.

However, it is precisely at this point that the problem of providence becomes most acute. The psalmist may regard doubts about God's providential way as stupid and ignorant, the mark of the beast (Ps. 73. 21f), yet the near scepticism of Ecclesiastes suggests that hard questions were being asked. To speak of God requiting the guilt of fathers upon their children recognizes the hard facts of heredity, and the difficulties are discussed by Jeremiah and Ezekiel in terms of sour grapes. Further, if God hardens men in sin (as in Isa. 6. 10) and "has made everything for its purpose, even the wicked for the day of trouble" (Prov. 16. 4), how can he condemn them? If it is all the penalty for sin, "why should a living man complain . . . about the punishment of his sins?" (Lam. 3. 39). Clearly there is recognition that providence has its negative evidences.

But what of the suffering of the innocent? This is the poignant problem, challenging the concept of a moral order under a God who is both good and almighty, and the more acute the closer providence is related to the individual. It is important to recognize that this is a problem only where there is a belief in providence. For those who move in the context of fate or *maya* or *karma-samsara* there is no such problem. Where, however, there is belief in divine providential care of the individual, the suffering of the innocent, whether or not exacerbated by the sight of the prosperity of the evil (Ps. 73. 3), offers the sharpest challenge—"even God's providence seeming estranged".

Although there was never a time when some were not tempted to say "my steps had well-nigh slipped", it could be argued that, so long as it was held that the individual was so bound up with the family as to be regarded as surviving in it, "the instincts of justice were satisfied if the law of retribution and recompense could be traced in the destinies of the family";[6] but with the denial by the later prophets that children were punished for the parents' sins the problem could not be thus escaped.

It is often suggested that the problem is more acute in the Old Testament for the lack of any belief in a compensating life hereafter. Will not the righteous God deal with men according to their deserts? Apparently not, if it is in this world only that rewards and punishments come. Yet the fact that the Old Testament does not see an answer in terms of resurrection until Daniel should warn us against thinking of the immortal hope in terms of compensation. What the Old Testament has to say may be other than and less confident than what can be said in the light of the resurrection of Jesus, but what it does say is in terms of significance not comfort, as in Psalm 46 where the reality of God is affirmed beyond the most terrible calamities.

We have already argued that the biblical doctrine of providence takes account of what God does both in and to history. History is too complex to yield any simple moral view of the triumph of God over evil. There are tragic defeats (and the very essence of tragedy is the destruction of what ought not to be destroyed). Certainly the prophets found no unambiguous record of the victory of the good over evil. It is because history remains ambiguous and gives no clear idea of the triumph of God over evil that faith looks forward to final judgement and redemption. This is not to say that history is without meaning. It has many meanings, fulfilments, and judgements, but they are partial and point beyond themselves, revealing, as it were, God's *hidden* sovereignty over history.

Such an attitude is implicit in Jeremiah's combined declaration of faith and complaint (Jer. 12. 1ff; cf. Mark 9. 24). His words are a clear statement of the problem which exercised many. Thus the psalmist does not conceal the challenge to the doctrine of creation and providence on the evidence of the indifference and cruelty of nature, evil, suffering, and the triumph of wickedness. All in all, there is no disposition in the Old Testament to shirk the problem. Can it be said to deal effectively with it?

Job does not hesitate to credit God with responsibility for a long list of stumbling-blocks, but in 9. 24 he seems to pose the resultant

6 A. F. Kirkpatrick, *The Book of Psalms* (1897), p. 188.

problem in such a way as to show faith in all-embracing providence Psalm 62. 12 expresses the assurance found elsewhere that God will reward each man according to his deeds. In other places (e.g. Ps 52. 5ff; 92. 11) the punishment of the wicked is adduced as evidence of divine justice and Isaiah 26. 9 has more positive vindication of providence in the face of evil. Psalm 37 predicts that in the end the wicked will be destroyed and the good will enjoy everlasting happiness. But how many in the toils of hard experience believed that report?

"Blessed is the man whom thou dost chasten . . . and whom thou dost teach out of thy law." The idea that suffering may have educative value, expressed in Psalm 94. 12f and developed by Elihu in Job 32—37 represents a more solid approach than the scattered hints above. But it was (and is) an argument of limited value. Apart from the simple fact that it may bring more consolation to the doctor than to the patient, it seems to ignore the stark reality that much suffering does anything but ennoble. It is possible, with Job, to apply this interpretation in the light of experience, but it can hardly be put forward as a doctrine. It is often suggested that the furthest reach towards a solution of the problem in the Old Testament is found in Isaiah 52. 13—53. 12. Inasmuch, however, as this is part of the prophetic attempt to interpret the whole situation of the community under judgement in exile, it is better related to the study of historical experience touched on earlier. To deny any justification for seeing individual reference in this vision of the vicarious and redemptive potential of innocent suffering would be to reject a good deal of the New Testament; but discussion of that aspect is best deferred until we come to consider that great moment at which the idea was taken up and glorified in action.

Perhaps the most positive and hopeful line is that which begins to emerge in Psalm 73. There is full recognition of all the facts which test and challenge faith in divine providence. Then at verse 15 comes the realization that to react by concluding that it has no meaning is to break faith with the community. The conclusion comes in the assurance that no earthly happiness, present or to come, is comparable in value to fellowship with God. The hope that the ambiguities of the present will be overcome and eliminated in the future belongs to the realm of human ideas. The biblical view, embryonic in Psalm 73, appeals for validation of faith in providence not so much to the temporal future as to the eternity of value (cf. the use of αἰώνιος). No vicissitudes of history, no confusion of the contingencies of nature, no pressures of immediate human need, can finally triumph over the will of God to redeem.

The suggestion that God's will breaks in at points which man cannot overcome or transcend raises the allied problem of the relation of divine providence to human freedom. It may seem that, in the end, man's free will is illusion. Again, the Old Testament does not ignore or underestimate the problem. It may not succeed in working out the relation between the will and foreknowledge of God and human responsibility, but it never loses sight of either factor. Looking very broadly at the evidence we see how often the freedom and responsibility of man is stressed. How else can a man's prayers avail with God?[7] God has given man power to choose between good and evil, between obedience and disobedience, and constantly calls on him to exercise his choice (cf. the reiterated "Choose ye" of Deuteronomy). He has, indeed, so chosen to curtail his own power that man is able, temporarily at least, to thwart God's plans, even to burden him with his sins (Isa. 43. 22ff).

But the power remains with God. He sends both good and evil; blessing and calamity. The fortunes of his people and of each member are determined by the law of recompense. He directs the actions of men to his own ends

> A man's mind plans his way,
>   but the Lord directs his steps. (Prov. 16. 9)

So he can destroy the plans of the mighty. His action in and by men is through his spirit which both blinds and enlightens; both hardens in sin and renews in righteousness. In short, God is the potter and man the clay.

This metaphor crops up in many contexts, some non-biblical, in regard to divine omnipotence and control. An early and biblical use is found in Jeremiah 18 where, developing Genesis 2. 7, the prophet presents Yahweh as dealing with both Israel and the nations as a potter deals with his clay. In his hands man is fragile and dependent. Yet it is for man's good that the divine power is so used. If men fail to carry out what God plans it is not the end; he can begin again and remould the clay. We should not, however, so interpret the Pauline use in Romans 9—11 as to destroy all freedom in men. Paul, in fact, is using the figure to stress God's right and power to overrule the claims of racial privilege. The conclusion of the argument is to vindicate the justice and grace of God in the light of his total purpose.

There is no inclination in the Bible to regard the power of God as anything but overwhelming. There is, however, nothing to

---

[7] In his 1966 Hulsean Lectures, *Prayer and Providence* (1968), Peter Baelz has argued that petitionary prayer is the confluence of divine providence and human faith.

sanction the misuse of *omnipotens* so as to suggest one who can do
anything, even the impossible. That "all things are possible with
God" is intelligible in the context of Mark 10. 23ff but irrational
when made absolute. We do well to remember that the credal
"Almighty" derives from pointing to one able to make all in all
serve his will and purpose. Yet God does not force his will to
annihilate what opposes. Patient, he waits till the time is ripe. That
his long-term plans will be carried out in the end; that opposition
will ultimately be overthrown; that the pride and self-will of men
will be judged—of this biblical experience and witness is sure.
Berdyaev gathers together evidence which all in all neither com-
promises with fatalism nor disregards human freedom by concluding that in the biblical tradition "providence is neither necessity
nor compulsion; it is the continuous union of God's will and human
freedom".[8]

There is a further dimension to the problem which must be
mentioned even though it cannot be treated in full, the *cosmic*
character of sin and evil. This is fully recognized in the Bible.
Many illustrations could be given: free spiritual beings contending,
though never on equal terms, with God (e.g. Dan. 7. 21ff; 10. 13);
the demon-ridden background of the New Testament with Satan no
longer the agent of God but the hostile prince of this world; and
the struggle against spiritual powers described in Ephesians 6.
While it is never doubted that their final overthrow is sure, present
sufferings at their hands raise the question whether God is either
powerless or indifferent. Daniel's confession of faith reaches the
great conclusion: "Our God whom we serve is able to deliver us . . .
But if not . . . we will not serve your gods" (Dan. 3. 17f).

The citation from Daniel could have been used appropriately at
many points of our argument as typical of the biblical witness. It
may suggest that the *arguments* for providence are less strong than
the faith in it. We may approach our conclusion by stopping awhile
to consider the alternatives. Is it that events happen by chance or
at the *diktat* of fate? For the Persians, for example, man's lot was
linked with the movements of the stars, ruling all things, modifying
even what the gods provided. Whatever the Persian influence on
post-exilic thought that alternative offered little temptation. Later
the Qur'ān, developing the biblical tradition in its own way,
declares that "every nation has its appointed time and when their
appointed time comes they cannot keep it back an hour nor can
they bring it on" (7. 33). How this view applies to the individual
is illustrated by Mohammed's contemporary Zuhair: "I have seen

[8] Op. cit., p. 79.

doom let out in the dark like a blind camel; those it struck down died and those it missed lived to grow old." Accept the alternatives and you deny human freedom; reject them and what of divine omnipotence? The biblical writers never surrendered to the demands of a logic on which Islam was later to build. Typical of the biblical outlook is Jonah which ends, quite illogically, with the mercy of God on all his creatures: on the reluctant prophet wallowing in self-pity; on repentant Nineveh; on the ignorant masses and inanimate creation. It all points forward to the final disclosure of sovereign love—the two primary terms in the consideration of providence.

That God is "merciful and gracious, slow to anger, and abounding in steadfast love and faithfulness" (Exod. 34. 6) as declared in the Law is echoed widely in Prophecy and Psalm. The evidence we have briefly considered and illustrated. That the argument from creation and history is strong the New Testament does not deny; indeed it makes use of it. But it places less reliance on it in the light of its own *knowledge*—knowledge of the glory of God in the face of Jesus Christ (2 Cor. 4. 6); that God was in Christ reconciling the world to himself (2 Cor. 5. 19); that while we were yet sinners Christ died for us (Rom. 5. 8); that Christ who died for our sins was raised from the dead to become goodness in us (Rom. 4. 25). Therefore the witness of the New Testament is not simply to the love of God, nor simply that God loves (the Almighty the All-loving too)—but that God is love.

When thinking about providence there is always the temptation to claim too much. What has been written here may indicate that we shall find no confident answers to the recognized difficulties before and without the cross and the resurrection. Hence we ought not to underestimate the significance of this doctrine as distinctively *Christian*. We began by quoting Jesus' sure word, typical of teaching which expresses confidence in the providential care of God. Yet it is he himself who most clearly reveals providence. In him the divine life is lived in human form and experience. Herein he faced evil, endured its full power, and passed through death to resurrection. That victorious end to the truly earthly life is the assurance of the final triumph of the goodness of God.

Here we pick up an earlier reference to the need for the cross to control our thinking about providence—especially as touching the life of the individual when suffering. The great Servant Song of Isaiah underlines the perennial and universal problem presented by suffering. It is not natural for men to see meaning, let alone benefit, in suffering. It is the great stumbling-block. It is part of the greatness of the biblical witness that it never falls into the temptation to avoid the issue by assuming that suffering is unreal, but rather attempts somehow to bring it within the understanding of providence. The nearest approach to an answer is found in the principle of redemptive and vicarious suffering to which Isaiah 53 testifies.

> How the Servant can suffer for others, how he can endure the penal consequences of the sins of others—these are questions which Deutero-Isaiah does not raise. But we take the heart out of the words, and deprive the Servant of his noblest glory, if we look on his work as only an object-lesson, an incentive or even a piece of voluntary self-sacrifice : it is God who has brought him to stand where others should stand, to endure what others should endure; and he stands and endures because it is God's will for him, without complaint.[9]

It is precisely this way of bringing suffering within the divine ordering of life that we see manifest in him who "although he was Son, learned obedience through what he suffered" (Heb. 5. 8). It is in the light of this great fact that the last word of the Bible is to offer a confidence in divine providence which no disaster can break.

In the end the Bible is not concerned with particular or special "providences" involving some kind of special and miraculous intervention into the course of events. It is concerned with the assurance of the never failing providence of God such as we find in Romans 8. 31ff. Here is the perfect and classical expression of the Christian meaning of the term. Paul's confidence does not mean that we may not die or suffer catastrophe or even that our confidence in God may not be threatened by changes of fortune. He makes clear that if we are to distinguish between what is legitimate and what is illusory in our thinking about providence we have to recognize a basic distinction in the character of God. He is revealed in the Bible as both Law and Freedom. His character is partly but not wholly revealed in the structure of the universe, in the basic laws of life. Thus when John declares that the world was made by Christ and that he is the pattern on which human life is moulded, he is declaring that love is the law of life. In the same way Paul reaches the climax of his doctrine of providence in the confident triumphant persuasion that no evil shall prevail against the love which creates, sustains, and orders all things.[10]

John Burnaby reminds us that "without the symbolism of warfare, of struggle and victory, our picture of the Christian life would be incomplete. But the comparison breaks down at the

[9] J. K. Mozley, *The Doctrine of the Atonement* (1915), p. 29.

[10] For a development of the argument see A. N. Whitehead's analysis of religious experience and its implications concerning God and the moral order of the world in *Religion in the Making* (1926).

crucial point, for all the fighting of this world is with the weapon of force. Love never forces, and therefore there can be no certainty that it will overcome. But there may, and there must, be an unconquerable hope."[11] This is deeply relevant to our theme, especially when we remember how the New Testament sets all the judgements of God in history against the hope of final judgement and redemption. We have already had reason to stress that in the Bible hope is related not simply to the future in time but rather to eternity. The eternity to which New Testament hope looks and faith appeals is not some undifferentiated eternity which removes all the distinctions of good and evil in history. The God revealed in the Bible both has freedom over history and is engaged in history. When he comes down in Christ he cannot deal with the evil in history except by taking it in and on himself. It is precisely this genius for being involved in, yet transcending, the vicissitudes of history which distinguishes the religion of the Bible from this-worldly religions which look for the meaning of history within the historical process and the other-worldly religions which flee history for some passionless eternity. It is the biblical under-standing of providence which encourages us to take seriously the warfare of which Burnaby speaks, and also provides resource against despair when the struggle seems not to avail. "Godliness is of value in every way," as Paul reminds Timothy, "as it holds promise for the present life and also for the life to come" (1 Tim. 4. 8).

"There is none other that fighteth for us, but only thou, O God." This declaration of the 1662 Prayer Book may be said to be a not inadequate summing up of what the Bible means by providence. That there are dangers and limitations, however, seems to have occurred to the Revisers of 1928 with their alteration to "none other that ruleth the world". This we can accept so long as we remember that "He reigneth from the Tree".

[11] *Amor Dei* (1938), p. 318.

3

THE IDEA OF PROVIDENCE
IN OTHER RELIGIONS

GEOFFREY PARRINDER

Many standard works of Christian theology have references to providence in the index, but many books on other religions make no such reference. Perhaps then this is one of the distinctive beliefs of Christianity; an advantage if one holds a personal theism, or a sign of weakness if the rule of *karma* or law is taken to be universal and independent of religion as some modern Buddhist apologists say.

It is difficult to find a general treatment of this subject; but, although some of the contributions to the *Encyclopaedia of Religion and Ethics* are out of date, it has an interesting article on providence. Here it is said that "in a very wide sense" some such idea as providence "would seem to be indispensable to religion". Unfortunately the article then restricts itself to Hebrew and Christian ideas, and for the rest of mankind it is content to remark that "in Buddhism and some forms of pantheism—the word 'providence' cannot legitimately be used as of a relation between 'God' and 'the world'."[1] This is a very large exception—some would say up to half the world—and it might seem to invalidate the original claim that faith in providence is essential to religion. But perhaps the definition of "God" needs considering more closely in eastern religions, and also some of the implications of ideas of providence.

Islam

At least those non-Christian religions which teach a personal theism may be expected to have the idea of providence, and the clearest example is Islam. The Qur'ān is the basic scripture and source,

---

[1] *E.R.E.*, Vol. x (1918), article by W. T. Davison.

whether Muhammad wrote it or simply dictated it. It is both exhortation and religious experience from a thoroughly Semitic context, and one of the longest personal religious writings among the world's scriptures.

The fundamental declaration of Islam is the confession of faith: "There is no god but God". Allāh was the proper name of God, and with characteristic religious genius Muhammad adopted the Allāh of the Meccans as the only real deity. Allāh is like Yahweh in the Old Testament, not like Elohim to which the word may be related in form, for Allāh has no plural and is the personal name of God. This rather remote deity of Mecca became to Muhammad the mighty and omnipresent God, nearer to man "than the vein in his neck" (Qur'ān, sūra 50. 15).

The character of God is revealed in many divine epithets, the Most Beautiful Names. Most of them are found in the Qur'ān; later, under Indian influence, they began to be recited on prayer beads and are chanted all over the Islamic world down to this day. A title that is usually translated as Provider (*ar-razzāq*) occurs only once (51. 58), but the belief in the dependence of all creation upon the provision of God is very common. God is called the Bestower of gifts, Patron, Generous, Helper, Protector, Enricher, Governor, and Kind—a common title.

It is well known that Islam dislikes the name Father for God, though the Qur'ān does not forbid its use. Similarly the idea of the love of God was originally weak, though the Ṣūfī mystics later made much of it. Rahbar maintains that "unqualified Divine Love for mankind is an idea completely alien to the Qur'ān. In fact 'to love' is too strong a phrase to convey the idea . . . which can be rendered equally well as 'to like or to approve'." Even if the translation "love" is adopted occasionally, yet "nowhere do we find the idea that God loves mankind. God's love is conditional. He loves those who do good, those who turn repentant to him."[2] These are strong words and need some qualification.

Although the God of Islam is high and lifted up, yet his commonest attributes are mercy and compassion. At the head of every chapter in the Qur'ān but one is the ascription to God "the Merciful, the Compassionate" (*ar-Rahmān ar-Rahīm*), or the Compassionate Compassionator. Ar-Rahmān seems to have been Muhammad's own innovation when used as a proper name equivalent to Allāh. Commentators say that the mercy of God was universal, extended to believers and unbelievers as a Quranic verse remarked: "Verily thy Lord is bounteous towards the people, but most of them do not show gratitude" (27. 75).

[2] D. Rahbar, *God of Justice* (1960), pp. 172f.

With all these epithets about the creation, power, and compassion of God, it would seem that God does everything and needs no intermediaries. Yet angels and messengers are often mentioned in the Qur'ān; Gabriel and Michael are named, and they must have formed a part of the early tradition. But the false gods are nothing or powerless; they cannot even create a fly and are "only names which you and your fathers have named" (22. 72; 12. 40). Muhammad's belief was thoroughly theocentric and he has been called a God-intoxicated man, like Boehme or Blake. God was the overpowering reality for him, and he was not concerned with logical consistency for his faith.

The providence of God is demonstrated in the Qur'ān in stories of the creation. God created the heavens and the earth in six days without being affected by fatigue (50. 37). Or he created the earth in two days, and bestowed blessing upon it, and decreed the foods in it in four days (41. 8f). God made man from clay, set the earth for cattle, and made fruit, palm trees, grain, and herbs. And after each enumeration of the acts of God, on earth and in paradise, this chapter has a constant refrain, "Which then of the benefits of your Lord will you count false?" (55. 12ff).

God provides also for animals. "How many a beast bears not its own provision, but God provides for it and for you." This is because God is the one who hears and knows, and he makes "generous provision" according to his will, because he knows everything (29. 60f). Since God gives freely to all, he has a claim on human gratitude. "Ingratitude" is *kufr*, which later meant "unbelief"; the *kāfir* is the ingrate who conceals God's blessings, and so becomes the infidel.

The Qur'ān is not an autobiography of Muhammad, whose name occurs in it only four times, though much of it is addressed to and through him. But there are references to his experiences of revelation, from God or Gabriel: "taught by One strong in power, forceful; he stood straight upon the high horizon, then he drew near and let himself down, till he was two bow-lengths off or nearer, and suggested to his servant what he suggested" (53. 5ff). There is certainly a personal providence in the moving words which refer to the unhappy childhood of the orphan Muhammad: "Did he not find thee an orphan and give thee shelter? Did he not find thee erring and guide thee? Did he not find thee poor and enrich thee?" (93. 6f). The conclusion is that the Prophet also must be kind to orphans and beggars, and declare the goodness of the Lord.

Personal providence is assumed for all believers in the Fātiha, the opening prayer that forms part of every act of worship during the day. Here God is appealed to for help and guidance: "Thee do we serve, and on thee do we call for help; guide us on the straight path" (1. 4f). The straight path is the simple and direct way of the service of God, which is not only belief but right conduct.

In Hebrew and Christian thought providence is seen in salvation history not only in the lives of individuals but in society or race or Church; and it is sometimes said that this idea of sacred history is peculiar to the Jewish–Christian world outlook. But Kenneth Cragg, in his recent Jordan lectures, has asserted that there is a sacred history in the Qur'ān.[3] Faced with the Jews and Christians, with their prophets and scriptures which he acknowledged as divinely sent, Muhammad asserts that now God has sent his word to the Arab people in their own language, and by their own prophet. "Verily we have sent it down as an Arabic Qur'ān" (12. 2). God has sent others messengers before, giving them wives and children, and none of them could produce a sign without the permission of God. For every term there was a book, but with God is "the Mother of the Book", the heavenly archetype of all scripture (13. 37f).

The sense of being a chosen people was strengthened by the Migration (*Hijra*) of Muhammad and his followers to Medina. In the ensuing struggles with the Meccan armies the Muslims were victorious at Badr (A.D. 624), but defeated at Uhud (A.D. 625), though not decisively. Finally, in only eight years Muhammad rallied most of Arabia to his cause and conquered Mecca itself. The first victory was a "sign" from God; "God has already helped you at Badr, when you were insignificant" (3. 119). When the Muslims called upon God for help, he responded by saying, "I am going to reinforce you with a thousand of the angels as auxiliaries" (8. 9). This verse may have been meant as an encouragement after the defeat of Uhud, which shook the faith of some Muslims. It raised the problem of suffering more seriously than in the earlier persecutions. This is blamed, as in the Bible, upon the weakness of men, "you flinched and vied in withdrawing from the affair"; or it was the devil, "it was Satan who sought to trip them up"; or there came a divine trial, "then he turned you from them, that he might try you"; or the defeat was a punishment, "so he recompensed you with distress upon distress" (3. 145ff). The conclusion of the Prophet, to rally his dispirited followers, was that God is forgiving and kindly and loves those who trust him, for if God helps you no one can overcome you.

The Migration to Medina, which so properly marks the beginning of the Islamic era from A.D. 622, established the community of

---

[3] K. Cragg, *The Privilege of Man* (1968), pp. 103ff.

Muslims, "submitters" to God. This community was above all clan and tribal loyalties or divisions, and it was a great challenge to current Arabian ideas. The Bedouin were told to say, "we have become Muslims", and while the divine creation of "races and tribes" is recognized, yet "the most noble in the eyes of God is the most pious" (49. 13f).

Many of the teachings of Islam were in radical opposition to the ethical as well as to the religious ideas of the Bedouin. Islam sought to level down social differences and genealogical rivalries. The mockings and boastings of the tribes were to cease, and in Islam there was to be no distinction of rank between Arabs and others. All Muslims were brothers, and in the "community [*umma*] of Muhammad" all distinctions were banned as relics of the times of ignorance before the coming of Islam. The refuge which Christian Ethiopia had provided to persecuted Muslims ensured that dark-skinned people would be respected, and before long Muhammad was proclaimed as "the prophet of white and black men". Muhammad taught the Bedouin that forgiveness was not a weakness but a virtue, and retaliation was evil. There was plenty of opposition to the ascetic practices of Muhammad, the irksome frequent prayers, restrictions on sexual relationships, and a total ban on drinking intoxicants. Some of the most surprising conscientious objectors of history were those who, for centuries, composed poems in praise of wine and went to prison rather than give up their drink.[4]

The community of Islam triumphed, the religion became universal, and in its early days it spread more rapidly and successfully than any other religion has done. Within a hundred years from the death of Muhammad in 632 the Islamic embassies reached as far as China in the east, and in the west Islamic armies were fighting in the heart of France. To the faithful the victories of the religion were evidence that God had signally blessed his people.

Cantwell Smith suggests that part of the trouble of the Islamic world today is the spiritual disturbance and uncertainty caused by the break up of Islamic power. The Golden Age of Islam ended with the fall of the Arab empire to the Mongols in the thirteenth century, and men look back to those wonderful times. But the new rulers were or became Muslims, and the Turkish empire lasted till the present century. Then the Sick Man of Europe broke down, the empire was fragmented into western colonies or nation states which show few signs of unity, and Turkey itself has become a secular state. What has happened? Has God deserted his people? Why do the Nazarene or ungodly Westerners triumph over all the world?

---

[4] I. Goldziher, *Muslim Studies* (E.T. 1967), pp. 24ff, 54ff.

Why do they despise the Arabs as backward or lazy and favour the Jews? There is a severe problem for belief in the providential guidance and blessing of God. The solution given by fundamentalists, like the Wahhābī of Arabia, is that Muslims have been unfaithful and should return to the purity of the faith. Modernists try to adopt many western ways, while remaining Muslims. Ordinary people practise the ancient faith, and leave the problems to the inscrutability of God.[5]

This raises the problem of the so-called fatalism of the Islamic peoples, or of all orientals, who are supposed to believe so firmly in Kismet or destiny that they fold their arms and watch the West going ahead without complaint. How can such fatalism, if it is such, be squared with any kind of belief in providence? It is a problem, of course, for other religions that believe in the omnipotence and justice of God, and also in his care for mankind.

The Qur'ān does not doubt the omnipotence and directing rule of God, and several verses say that God leads some men aright and leads others astray. But the Qur'ān is a book of religion rather than systematic theology and, like the Bible, it is not afraid of paradox. After all, Isaiah attributed good and evil to the creation of God (Isa. 45. 7), and the Lord's Prayer asks God to "lead us not into temptation". The *Encyclopaedia of Islam* says that "antinomies had no terrors for Muhammad. He, evidently, never thought about predestination and free will, whatever later traditions may have put into his mouth; he expressed each side as he saw it at the moment, and as the needs of the moment stood. So Allāh is kind, loving, patient on one side, and ... again he is the Haughty, the Tyrant."[6]

The problem of the divisions and unbelief of men clearly worried Muhammad, but it was referred back to the will of God. So in one verse he says, "If God had so willed, he would have made you one community, but he leads astray whom he will and guides whom he will" (16. 95). But in another verse where the same question is raised the divisions are said to occur "in order that he may try you". And rather than propose a passive acceptance, men are urged to "strive to be foremost in what is good" (5. 53). Therefore along with insistence upon the omnipotence of God the Qur'ān constantly exhorts men to be active in belief and good works.

How to reconcile omnipotence and free will, and transcendence and immanence, was left by Muhammad to his successors. The Traditions, which have played a large part in the history of thought, but are now severely criticized, reflect the struggles of the early years of Islam. Some Traditions say that Muhammad objected to

[5] W. C. Smith, *Islam in Modern History* (1957), pp. 28ff, 94ff.
[6] *Shorter Encyclopaedia of Islam* (1953), p. 35.

any discussions of theological questions, while others fathered long stories on the Prophet in support of their views. Many orthodox teachers disliked attempts at rational justification of revealed religion, and there is a dreadful Tradition which shows how far belief in predestination could be taken. It is said that at the creation God took from the loins of Adam two handfuls, white and black, which were all the future generations of men. And he said of the white and black respectively, "These are in Paradise, and I care not; and these are in Hell, and I care not."[7]

Against such monstrous Traditions of the God who does not care arose first the Mu'tazila, who said that if God decreed infidelity he would himself be an infidel, and that God ought to guide all men to good. The orthodox objected to the application of "ought" to God, and eventually their champion al-Ash'arī propounded the way of compromise. God is the only creator and actor, and man has no power. "We affirm that God determines our works and creates them as determined for us", and yet man can "acquire" or "appropriate" actions, and so he has some responsibility.[8]

More important and lasting than the Mu'tazila were the Ṣūfīs. Not much concerned with problems of creation, they were intent upon close personal relationships with God, and they early spoke of the love of God in ways that owed something to Christian mystics. However, the extreme transcendentalism of the orthodox turned in Ṣūfism to extreme immanentalism, and this easily became a monistic identification with God. Ḥallāj spoke of God as Father, and used a word for "incarnation" (*ḥulūl*) which most mystics rejected. But he so identified himself with God that he was crucified for declaring, "I am the Truth", a title of God.[9]

We cannot stay on the great field of Ṣūfism, but its persistent appeal shows a warmer appreciation of the nature of God than is found in the orthodox rigidity. The ordinary Muslim may say, "it is the will of God", when all else has failed, but he will usually try anything once, and go to hospitals or holy men for cure from physical and spiritual ills.

Hindu Theism

Modern Indian apologetic often claims that the true Hindu religion is monism, which is a universal "perennial philosophy", and that therefore beliefs in a personal God, Providence, and I–Thou relationships, are rather childish. But this monism has never been the religion of the mass of Hindus or of many of the leading thinkers.

[7] R. A. Nicholson, *The Idea of Personality in Ṣūfism* (1923), p. 23.
[8] R. J. McCarthy, *The Theology of al-Ash'arī* (1953), pp. 74f.
[9] L. Massignon, trs., *Le Dīwān d'al-Ḥallāj* (1955), pp. 17, 92f.

The most ancient Hindu scriptures, the hymns of the Rig Veda, are psalms addressed to many gods, deities of heaven and earth and the elements, dating from about 1500 B.C. The dominant god is Indra, who is storm and warrior and national deity, a hard-drinking Yahweh. But ritual gods, Agni the fire and Soma the sacred drink, are also very prominent. With Agni appears a henotheism, or identification with other divinities, in which he is called also Indra, Vishnu, and other gods. Although many Vedic hymns seem barbarous, yet the gods are both terrifying and helpful. Indra is called "better than a father, like a mother" (Rig Veda 4, 17, 17), and Agni is called "father, mother, brother and friend for ever" (6, 1, 5; 10, 7, 3).

The Vedic hymns are psalms to the gods, but little is recorded by way of reply. There is no "thus saith the Lord", for God never spoke to man in the Vedas. The traffic is godward and not the reverse. Yet no doubt the gods were believed to answer the many prayers that were directed to them, and they were kindly to their worshippers. An idea close to that of providence appears in verses about creation in the tenth and last book of the Rig Veda. Here the All-maker, Viśva-karman, is wise and mighty, creator and highest. He is also "our Father, our Creator, and Disposer . . . to him other beings go to ask him" (10, 82, 3). But a diversion towards the search for an impersonal principle behind all things appeared in a famous concluding hymn of questioning. In the beginning, it is said, there was neither existence nor non-existence, and who truly knows whence this creation was produced? "Whence this creation came into being, whether it was established [by God?] or whether not—only he who is its overseer in the highest heaven knows, or perhaps he does not know!" (10, 129).

The Upanishads continued this speculation. In the beginning there was nothing at all, in the beginning this was the Self alone, in the begining this was Brahman. Then the Vedic gods are thinned down from 3,306 to one, and that one is Brahman, the Holy Power. The only duality that remained was between the divine and the human, and in nine examples their unity was demonstrated, each one ending with the phrase "Thou art That". This is the charter of monism, the identity of the soul and God, though its interpretation has been much discussed and often modified.

These philosophical theories did not leave much room for providence, but it is evident from the Great Epic that there was a good deal of personal theism and polytheism going on all the time. Even towards the end of the classical Upanishads, philosophical dialogues though they may be, there are signs of the need for divine grace and kindness. The Śvetāśvatara Upanishad asks bluntly,

"What is the cause? whence are we born? on what are we established? overruled by whom, in pains and pleasures, do we live our various conditions, O ye theologians?" (1, 1). Finally it comes to a thoroughly theistic answer to the problems of creation, rejecting the theories of nature, time, or accident. "Some sages discourse of inherent nature; others likewise, of time. Deluded men! It is the greatness of God in the world by which this Brahma-wheel is caused to revolve" (6, 1). God is identified with Rudra, a Vedic storm God; he is transcendent, the origin of all, and he is asked to reveal himself as "auspicious" (*śiva*, the name of his god later). God "stands opposite creatures", he is lord of the worlds, and the great-souled man will show great love (*bhakti*) to his God (6, 23).

God did not speak to man in the Vedas, and, as far as the Upanishads are monistic, there was no room for conversation or much description of a deity who is "without qualities". The few traces of grace that appear are like bolts from the epic blue. But in the long Indian epics, the lush eighteen or more Purāṇas, and the countless medieval mystics who worshipped Vishnu or Śiva, there is a wealth of personal theism. This appears most clearly, finely, and influentially, in the Bhagavad-Gītā, the Song of the Lord Krishna, in the sixth book of the great epic Mahābhārata.

The Gītā is both conciliatory of different opinions and original in some doctrines. At first, and in various later verses, it seems to adopt the monism of the Upanishads, but very soon the personal character and concern of God appear. The Gītā is a long dialogue of the warrior Arjuna with his charioteer, the god Krishna, and most of it is explanation and exhortation from Krishna. Here God speaks almost for the first time in India, and he is a God of grace, who exercises providential care. Krishna is called "the Father of this world, the Mother, the Establisher, the Grandsire"; he is also "the Goal, Supporter . . . Dwelling-place, Refuge and Friend" (9, 17f). These titles are repeated later and there is no doubt both of the transcendence and kindliness of the deity (11. 43f).

One of the great teachings of the Gītā is the necessity for action, instead of ascetic withdrawal or idleness. And the appeal for action is strengthened by the example of God himself. "For me there is nothing unattained to gain, and yet I still continue in action, for if I did not . . . men would follow my way . . . and I should be the agent of their destruction" (3, 22f). This teaching of divine activity is reinforced by the doctrine of incarnation or *avatāra*. "Whenever there is a languishing of Righteousness and a growth of Unrighteousness, then I send myself forth." This is done "for the protection of the good, and the destruction of evildoers" (4, 7f).

It can be debated how far this is a real "incarnation", in the sense of God becoming a true man, for even in his human form Krishna has four arms. Yet there is no doubt that the Gītā teaches the entry of God into the world, at least as a theophany, or series of appearances. Dasgupta, in his great critical history of Indian philosophy, pays tribute to the Gītā as the first to teach the incarnation of God. But he notes that the author of this scripture does not seem to be aware of the difficulty of combining the idea of God as unmanifested and undifferentiated with an incarnation as a man. It is fine that God should come to earth whenever righteousness is declining; but, if all good and evil emanate from God, why should he trouble himself when there is a disturbance of Righteousness? And is this disturbance not natural and divine?[10]

The Gītā's problem arises first of all from the clash of monism and incarnation, but it is further complicated by its teaching of transcendence. In the tenth chapter monism seems to be pushed almost to extremes by identifying Krishna with everything else in heaven and earth, and even with his hearer Arjuna; but the reverse is not stated, Arjuna is not Krishna. Then the very next chapter contains the most terrifying vision of transcendent deity in religious literature. Krishna is transfigured as the All-God, the Primal Deity, First Creator, greater than Brahman, the supreme resting-place of the universe. He is also a frightening deity, with countless eyes and mouths, bellies, arms and feet, and into his great maw all men are rushing to be absorbed or crushed. Arjuna is terrified at this vision and, significantly, he remembers that he may have been over-familiar with the human Krishna, in play or rest, sitting or eating, and so he begs for forgiveness. Arjuna pleads for grace, asking God to be to him "as father to his son, as friend to friend, as lover to beloved" (11, 44). So far the love has been on the human side, *bhakti* (devotion) demanded by the deity; but now the Lord shows his grace and comforts the terrified devotee. It is notable that the following chapter insists on devotion or love; not only is love asked from man, but in five successive verses the devotee is said to be "dear" to God, and in the last verse to be "dear beyond measure". This declaration of divine concern is only surpassed towards the end of the last chapter, where the devotee is "greatly loved" by God (18, 64).

Dasgupta says again that "the Gītā does not know that pantheism and deism and theism cannot well be jumbled up into one as a consistent philosophic creed".[11] But he agrees that the Gītā is a book of religion, which combines different conceptions of God without feeling the need to reconcile them. Its concern is to deliver

[10] S. Dasgupta, *A History of Indian Philosophy* (1932), ii, p. 533.
[11] Ibid., p. 527.

the divine message, and to show that God is the object of personal
devotion and the giver of gracious relationships.

There is a belief in the providence of God in the Gītā, in the
divine concern for man and his Avatar to restore righteousness. In
the development of the Krishna cult, and also in that of Rāma as
another gracious Avatar, the kindly relationship of God (Vishnu,
the deity behind the Avatars) is fundamental. In the later Purānas,
and in medieval poetry, much erotic symbolism was used of Krishna
and Rādhā, or God and the soul, far more lavish than that of the
Song of Songs. This is a vast field which cannot be sketched here,
and it must suffice to say that innumerable millions of Hindus have
never doubted the love of God in his Avatars. The followers of
Śiva, who had few or no Avatars, developed one of the purest forms
of monotheism in India, in which the deity was often said to appear
to the faithful in grace and compassion.

Theism alone was not enough to give men the assurance of the
kindly nature of the deity; but *bhakti* religion, whether to Vishnu or
Śiva, made an invaluable contribution to Hindu thought. In the
Mahābhārata one of the major themes is the struggle of Yudhish-
thira, the King of Righteousness (*dharma-rāja*), for his throne. Driven
away by his rivals with his wife Draupadī he wanders about in
adversity, while his wife is assailed with doubts not unlike those of
Job. She quotes an "ancient" story that "the world lies in the
power of its Lord . . . the Creator bestows of his own accord . . .
weal and woe". Man has no self-determination, and the Lord "plays
with his creatures as a child with his toys. The Creator does not bear
himself towards his creatures as a mother or a father would . . . I
rebuke the Creator who regards personality so unjustly." Yudhish-
thira is horrified at this blasphemy, but he remains firm in his own
faith because the new God of *bhakti* is gracious. So he tells his wife
not to "cast away God, the Creator of all beings . . . he, through
whose grace the *bhakta* enters into the freedom of death, he is the
highest Deity."[12]

Other strands of Indian thought tended to run counter to love or
providence, and in particular the doctrine of *karma*. Karma is
"action" or "act" in general (from a root *kri*, perhaps related to our
word "create"). Every action has a result, good or bad, and this
natural law is applied rigidly to the moral world. It became axiom-
atic to the Hindus that each state of existence of an individual is
conditioned by the morality of previous states, and very early this
doctrine was applied to successive lives on earth. In a well-known
passage in the first Upanishad, when a sage was asked where a man

[12] Version from R. Otto, *India's Religion of Grace and Christianity* (E.T.
1930), pp. 25f, 113f.

s when he is dead, he took his friend aside and they discussed the problem. "What they said was *karma*. A man becomes good by good *karma*, and evil by evil *karma*." In the next Upanishad the famous verse appears which says that those whose conduct on earth has been good will be reborn into the highest castes, while those whose conduct has been evil will be reborn as outcastes or animals.[13]

Karma acts automatically, though, when its entail is exhausted, men can improve their lot by good deeds. But there seems to be no room for a loving God and no escape from some kind of *karma*, good or bad, which binds man to this world and prevents him from attaining salvation or liberation. Ascetics, like the Jains, held that the only escape from *karma* was by complete inactivity, ultimately suicide. But the author of the Bhagavad-Gītā has some different and ingenious solutions. The Gītā shows that action is not wrong in itself, but only in the desire that seeks after fruits, rewards, or avoidance of punishments. So a man must act, perform his proper duty, but in a spirit of detachment from rewards. Then very early the Gītā adds a further point. Not only should one act without seeking rewards, one should act looking to God : "restraining his senses, disciplined, intent on me" (2, 61). This theistic teaching develops with increasing strength as the poem proceeds. In chapter six the simple description of meditation might be Buddhist, except for the final verse which is quite different and theistic : "controlling the mind, with his thoughts on me, let him sit disciplined and absorbed in me" (6, 14).

The gracious theism of the Gītā leads it right away from an automatic *karma*. God loves men in whatever way they come to him (4, 11), he is the Friend of every being (5, 29), their Saviour from the ocean of transmigration (12, 7), no devotee of his is lost, women and even outcastes who take refuge in him attain the highest goal, and, even if an evil-doer worships him with single devotion, he must be regarded as righteous after all (9, 30ff). The age-long popularity of the Gītā comes from this universal appeal, based on the divine concern for all creatures.

Buddhism

Not only popular Hindu religion but Indian philosophy is far from being all pantheism, and a personal theism which allows for provi-dence can be seen in classical philosophers like Rāmānuja and moderns like Aurobindo Ghose. But Buddhism seems to be quite

[13] Brihad-āranyaka Upanishad 3, 2, 13; Chāndogya Upanishad 5, 10, 7.

different, since it appears to have no supreme God in the strict sense.
Are there teachings in this religion also which can be considered
under the heading of providence?

The Buddha has often been called an atheist, or a "transtheist"
or "transpolytheist", by-passing the gods of his day. But his own
beliefs and those of his followers as presented in the texts pose complex problems. Gautama the Buddha did not deny the existence of
God, because a single Supreme Being was probably unknown to
India at his time. Lamotte, the great Belgian Buddhist scholar, says
that in all the Buddhist canon there is only one place where creation
by a Lord God is mentioned, but even there discussion centres on
the importance of action. It is even more remarkable that the
notion of an impersonal Brahman, so important in the Upanishads,
is unknown to the Buddhist texts. Either the Buddha knew nothing
of these discussions about Brahman, or he regarded them as too
speculative for his attention.[14]

Dislike of speculation is apparent in the early Buddhist scriptures,
and the Buddha mentioned questions that came to be called the Ten
Indeterminates. They were such problems as: Is the world eternal?
Is it finite? Is the soul the same as the body? Does one who has
gained the truth live again after death? and so on. The problem of
the existence of God is not found among these questions, but to all
those mentioned the Buddha said: "That is a matter on which I
have expressed no opinion, that question is not calculated to profit,
it is not concerned with Dharma, it does not help right conduct . . .
or Nirvāṇa."[15]

There are plenty of lesser gods, or "gentlemen" as Mrs Rhys
Davids called them, in the Buddhist canon. Brahmā, Vishnu, Indra,
and others appear frequently. But the gods act as a background for
the works of the Buddha; they are not helpers of men or givers of
salvation, which is obtained through the Buddha alone. He is the
"gods above the gods (*devātideva*)".

The Buddha's own faith is difficult to determine at this distance of
time from texts that were compiled centuries after his death and
altered freely by scribes. In the accounts of his Enlightenment he
says, "I directed my mind . . . knowledge came . . . light arose." But
the narratives were written by disciples to whom the Buddha was
a self-sufficient, supernormal, and celestial being. Some western
scholars say that the supernatural object set out by the Buddha was
Nirvāṇa, the changeless state beyond this world of change. Others
say that he believed in the eternal Dharma or Truth, which was

[14] E. Lamotte, *Histoire du Bouddhisme indien* (1958), p. 434 and T. W. Rhys
Davids, *Dialogues of the Buddha* (1899), i, p. 298.
[15] Rhys Davids, ibid., p. 187.

almost like God. Edward Conze says that the Buddha is "the personal embodiment of Nirvāna [and] becomes the object of all those emotions which we are wont to call religious".[16]

Buddhism is often presented to the West as a religion or morality of self-help and self-salvation, without all the superstitions of gods and the supernatural. Conze says that this misconception came from the agnostic or utilitarian prejudices of western scholars, who conscripted the Buddha into the tradition of British empiricism. But Buddhist salvation cannot come to the common man by himself, it demands the saving help of supernatural beings. "Bitter and incredible as it must seem to the contemporary mind, Buddhism bases itself first of all on the revelation of the Truth by an omniscient being, known as 'the Buddha'. . . . In all disputes the ultimate appeal is . . . not to the 'experience' of Tom, Dick and Harry, but to that of the fully enlightened Buddha."[17]

If there is no Supreme God, then, there is a substitute, the Supreme Buddha. Although past and future Buddhas are admitted, the Theravāda (Hīnayāna) Buddhists believe that Gautama is unique and supreme in this present very long world aeon. But Buddhists' dislike of speculation and their belief in a succession of creations and dissolutions which is held also by Hindus suggest that the Buddha does not seem to be a providential Creator. Creations and dissolutions of lives and universes go on eternally, and in ordinary life the law of *karma* holds. Since the soul appears to have been dispensed with, *karma* is the sole link between one life and another in the round of transmigration. Yet powerful religious beliefs, akin to providential care, enter in to complicate this simple moral law.

Although the Buddha is not an Avatar of the gods, since he is above all gods, yet he resembles the Hindu Avatars on a number of points. When he descends from heaven for his final incarnation, it is out of compassion for men. At his Enlightenment, instead of remaining in the bliss of Nirvāna, he sets out to preach to men from compassion. With the same motive he sends out his disciples, "for the happiness of the many, to take compassion on the world, to work profit and good, and happiness to gods and men".[18]

Even for the conservative Theravādins the Buddha is supreme, omniscient, all-seeing, Lord of Dharma, and no disciples have such titles. Every day the Theravādins use the Refuge Formula which begins, "I go to the Buddha for refuge". To follow Buddha is not merely an imitation, or a way of knowledge or morality, but it involves faith in the gracious supernatural being. "Such faith have

---

[16] E. Conze, *Buddhism* (1951), p. 40.
[17] E. Conze, *Buddhist Thought in India* (1962), p. 30.
[18] Dīgha Nikāya ii, 45ff.

I in the Exalted One, that I think there never has been, nor will there be, nor is there now any other . . . who is greater or wiser than the Exalted One."[19] This was said by early disciples, and much more would be said today.

The conservative Theravādins adore the Buddha in this manner, and the Mahāyāna go to far greater lengths. As northern Buddhism developed, stress was increasingly placed upon the compassion and care of the blessed Buddhas, plural now and active in many worlds at once. It was said to be a rule that they were devoted to the service of the world. "It is a rule" that three times by night and day they examine the world and ask: "Who is in pain, danger, or torment? Whom can I save from evil destiny to place him in heaven and deliverance?" Even if the sea could forget the time of the tide, the Buddha would never let the time pass for caring for his sons.[20]

In the Lotus Sūtra, cherished and recited by all Mahāyāna Buddhists, including Zen, there are countless Buddhas and Bodhisattvas, beings of compassion devoted to the care of all beings and saving them at their simple cries of faith. The Buddha himself is exalted with titles like the most supreme Hindu deities and Brahman. He is the Self-born, the Highest Spirit, the King of Righteousness, the Father of the World, the Refuge, Healer, and Protector of all creatures. He appears to show his kindness, to save all beings, to deliver those oppressed with suffering, and to produce among mortals gladness and joy.

The Bodhisattvas also are such objects of devotion that those who worship them attain enlightenment, and even little boys at play who make heaps of sand in their honour are saved. The favourite twenty-fourth chapter of the Lotus Sūtra is in honour of the Bodhisattva Avalokiteśvara (Kwanyin), who looks down in compassion on all men. Men who fall into any kind of danger have only to think of this gracious Bodhisattva to be delivered at once. "He with his powerful knowledge beholds all creatures who are beset with many hundreds of troubles and afflicted by many sorrows, and thereby is a Saviour in the world." He is a "protector, a refuge, a recourse in death, disaster, and calamity".[21]

Such kindly statements could be repeated endlessly. The Bodhisattvas took "ten inexhaustible vows" not to enter Nirvāṇa till all beings were saved. The *Path of Light*, which has been called a Buddhist *Imitation of Christ*, offers itself to all manner of suffering so that souls might gain salvation. These texts show clearly that

---

[19] Dīgha Nikāya iii, 99.
[20] Lamotte, *Histoire du Bouddhisme indien*, p. 714.
[21] Saddharma-puṇḍarīka 7, 34ff.; 15, 21; 24, 17ff.

Buddhism has a Supreme Being, or beings, gracious and helpful to men, a providence at least in the wide sense.

Other eastern religions cannot be considered here, but it appears to be true that some form of belief in providence is found in many religions, and is an essential ingredient of religion. Even those religions which are called "primitive", or pre-literate, are not simply based upon fear, but traces of divine goodness and grace are found in them. Further evidence of the widespread nature of such beliefs can be found in the *Festschrift* presented to E. O. James, entitled *The Saviour God*.

The idea of divine providence in history is particularly clear in Jewish–Christian traditions, and to a lesser degree in Islam, but it is not entirely absent elsewhere. In Buddhism and Hinduism the stories of the Buddha, and of the Avatars Krishna and Rāma, are recounted and cherished. Yet while these are illustrations of the power of the Buddha or of God, the legends are repetitive and the notion of the particularity of history is weak. The myths do not involve a providential ordering of human history, as in the Bible. Salvation is individual rather than social, and, although there are common eschatological beliefs in which the next Avatar or Buddha will restore the harmony of righteousness, this is part of the eternal round. It is impersonal and determined, and inconsistent with much of its own religion.

Mircea Eliade has written at great length upon universal ideas of sacred time and place, a sacredness repeated in rituals and myths, but he indicates the "very great religious revolution" in the biblical belief in the providential manner in which God "acts in history and enters into relations with historical beings".[22]

---

[22] M. Eliade, *Myths, Dreams and Mysteries* (E.T. 1968 edn), p. 153

4

WILLIAM PALEY:
OR THE EIGHTEENTH CENTURY
REVISITED

NORMAN GOLDHAWK

THE value of the eighteenth century in any discussion of the idea of providence is that its typical thinkers worked with concepts which, although they may be modified, cannot be entirely ignored by anyone at the present time. The eighteenth century, as is well known, inherited some striking changes in the intellectual climate, due to what was known as the New Philosophy, but which might also be called the New Science. Observations of facts had largely replaced deductions from arguments or hypothetical generalizations. Newton's conclusions had profound effects; but it was Locke who was to dominate European thought for more than a hundred years. "His work in conjunction with that of Newton created a new mentality among intelligent people, and instantly affected religious thought . . . The spirit in which he dealt with Christianity is more important than what he actually said about it. He made a certain attitude to religious faith almost universal."[1] As Mark Pattison remarked, the title of Locke's treatise, *The Reasonableness of Christianity* (1695), may be said to have been the solitary thesis of Christian theology in England for the greater part of a century.

Since it appeared that the laws of nature were the laws of reason, an emphasis upon nature is found everywhere in the eighteenth century. Although Leslie Stephen pointed out that the term "nature" introduces "as many equivocations as possible into all the theories, political, legal, artistic or literary, into which it enters",[2] what impressed the eighteenth century was not nature's

[1] G. R. Cragg, *The Church and the Age of Reason* (1960), p. 75.
[2] Cf. B. Willey, *The Eighteenth-Century Background* (1949), p. 2.

ambiguous aspect but its order and unity. Man might introduce disorder, and religion based upon revelation give rise to a confusing multiplicity of warring sects, each claiming finality, but nature, the expression of all that was orderly and rational, was the basis upon which all the religion, the ethics, the politics, the law, and the art of the future was to be constructed. Revelation might occur, but faith must first be firmly grounded in nature.

So the eighteenth century became an age of reason based upon faith, a confidence in the stability and regularity of the universal frame of nature, which was itself the expression of a Divine creative Mind. Accordingly, if an eighteenth-century writer set out to consider divine providence, it would be in terms which generally corresponded to this conviction. He was impressed by nature; as Locke wrote, "The works of nature everywhere sufficiently evidence a Deity". Professor Willey has drawn attention to the change which came over the eighteenth century in this respect, illustrated by John Ray's *The Wisdom of God in the Creation* (published in 1691, though written earlier), a book which became very popular during the century and which was used by both Wesley and Paley. Contrary to earlier emphasis upon the corrupting influences of the Fall, "nature is now to be contemplated as the finished and unimprovable product of divine wisdom, omnipotence and benevolence . . . God has placed man in a 'spacious and well-furnished world', and it is man's duty as well as privilege to exploit and improve it as much as he can . . . The world we are to exploit is no ruin, blasted by God's vengeance for mortal sin. It is the brave new world of science which lies before us."[3] This confidence in the rationality of nature will largely determine the approach to the problem of providence, and it explains the predilection for the argument from design for the existence of God. Even the enigmatic figure of Hume does not undermine this confidence in some purpose which is evidenced in nature, and in any case such a writer as Paley betrays no sign that Hume's scepticism had any effect upon him.

We should expect eighteenth-century writers therefore to see the workings of providence primarily in the general constitution and course of things, and this is what in fact we find. The world is orderly, subject to law, and its parts are wonderfully suited to each other. God's providence has provided it as a setting for man's moral discipline. It is a world admirably adapted to the purpose for which it was designed—that of providing the scene in which man prepares for a future state. The meaning of providence in general terms for the eighteenth century can be summed

[3] B. Willey, op. cit., pp. 35ff.

up as the provision by God in his benevolence of a beneficent constitution and course of events which provide the stage and the opportunity for man's preparation for a future life.

William Paley set out this view with great clarity. Although he wrote at the end of the century, he summed up many of the thoughts of his predecessors. He was Senior Wrangler at Cambridge and then Fellow and Lecturer at Christ's College, ending up as Archdeacon of Carlisle. He may not have been an original thinker, but he had great facility in expressing arguments already put forth. Most of his works were written as text-books: *Evidences of Christianity* (1794) was, for long, required reading at Cambridge. But of more immediate concern for the subject of this paper is his *Natural Theology, or Evidence of the Existence and Attributes of the Deity collected from the Appearances of Nature*, written in 1802. In concentrating very largely on this work, we need to remember that it would be unjust to assess his full thought as a Christian from it alone, since in it Paley kept strictly to the argument of a purely Natural Theology; his mature outlook certainly gave a more important place to revelation and the Christian dispensation than many earlier eighteenth-century writers. The book started with the well-known argument from design, illustrated by the watch. The works of nature display the same manifestation of design, only to a greater degree, and Paley proceeded to illustrated this at length by evidence from the varied organs and structures in animals, insects, and men, the constitution of plants, the uses of the basic elements of air, water, fire, and light, and the laws of astronomy. He concluded that the designer must have been a person, and that this person is God, a "perceiving, intelligent, designing Being, at the head of creation, and from whose will it proceeded". Further, God's attributes must be such as to account for the magnitude of his operation, and so we may speak of his omnipotence, omniscience, omnipresence, eternity, self-existence, necessary existence, and spirituality; all of these are explained in terms of natural theology alone. For example, the divine omnipresence is based upon the fact that everywhere laws of nature prevail, and law must be referred to an agent; so God who upholds everything by his power is everywhere present. Similarly, the proof of the unity of the Deity derives from the one plan which is observable through the universe: everywhere the same laws and systems prevail.

More germane to the subject of providence is Paley's concern with the divine goodness. He believed that this could be established solely by observation of nature. Two propositions can be asserted. First, "that in a vast plurality of instances in which contrivance is perceived, the design of the contrivance is *beneficial*". The constitution of animals shows how benevolent creation is.

> It is a happy world after all. The air, the earth, the water, teem with delighted existence. In a spring noon, or a summer evening, on whichever side I turn my eyes, myriads of happy beings crowd upon my view . . . Swarms of new-born flies are trying their pinions in the air. Their sportive motions, their wanton mazes, their gratuitous activity, their continual change of place without use or purpose, testify their joy, and the exultation which they feel in their lately discovered faculties (ch. xxvi).

This satisfactory state is not confined to the young. The great Parent of creation has provided that happiness is found with the purring cat, no less than with the playful kitten; in the arm-chair of dozing age, as well as in the animation of the chase. Indeed, the young are happy only when enjoying pleasure, but the old are happy when free from pain, and this state of ease is generally speaking more attainable than a state of pleasure. In his serene and dignified state, placed as it were on the confines of two worlds, the mind of a good man reviews what is past with the complacency of an approving conscience, and looks forward with humble confidence to the mercy of God and with devout aspirations towards his eternal and ever-increasing favour.

If one objects that Paley has selected only favourable instances of a beneficent creation, he will point out that every case he has described could be multiplied by millions. Taking natural life as a whole the preponderance is greatly in favour of happiness. If the situation of the human species is more doubtful, even there the preponderance of good over evil and of health over sickness is indicated by the attention which calamities excite. Happiness is the rule, misery the exception. Indeed, we are normally insensitive to the goodness of the Creator because of the sheer extensiveness of his bounty. We refer to special favours as blessings, whereas it is the common benefits of our nature which most properly ought to be accounted blessings of providence. The more common any good thing is, the more ought the bounty of the Donor to be recognized, for it exists in greater extent, even if we ourselves do not possess it. Surveying life as a whole Paley is certain that God, when he created the human species, wished their happiness. The ends for which all things were designed are good. Evil exists, but it is never the *object* of contrivance. Some things which men have created are intended to hurt or harm, like instruments of torture; but nothing of this sort is to be found in the works of nature. Paley is not unaware that venomous animals and the preying of creatures upon one another are apparent exceptions. Yet both features are the works of design. The fangs of vipers belong essentially to their constitution; we cannot accordingly say the effect was not intended. Nevertheless, in view of what we know of the goodness of creation as a whole, we ought to presume that, if we could survey the whole of the picture, even this arrangement, apparently so unpleasant, could be vindicated. Indeed, there is more to be said, for from the point of view of the particular animals the possession of hostile contrivances is a good thing. As to the preying of animals upon one another, can this rightly be termed evil? Animal life must end by some means; three methods bring this about—disease, decay, and violence. In their natural state animals are rarely subject to disease, nor would it be an improvement if they were. To leave animals to perish by decay would be miserable indeed. Would we alter the present system of pursuit and prey and see the world filled with drooping, superannuated, half-starved, helpless, and unhelped animals? Moreover, the fact that animals live in a state of alert because of danger promotes their general well-being and enjoyment. Paley argues further that the super-fecundity of animals is a beneficent arrangement, and at the same time it must obviously be kept in check. He devotes considerable space to the problem of animals devouring one another because he believes it is the chief, if not the only, instance in the works of the Deity in which the design may be called in question.

The second proposition which Paley put forward to assert God's beneficent providential government is also characteristic of his utilitarianism. It is, "that the Deity has added pleasure to animal sensations, beyond what was necessary for any other purpose, or when the purpose, so far as it was necessary, might have been effected by the operation of pain". The animal creation, Paley thinks, might have existed and continued to function quite apart from happiness or pleasure. Why add pleasure to the act of eating when the animal might have been impelled by the pain of hunger only to exert its organs and eat? So with the other senses; there could have been hearing without harmony and vision without beauty. Here is a constitution which demonstrates the pure benevolence of the Creator.

From these considerations Paley concluded that we can ascribe to the Deity the character of infinite benevolence. As to the existence of pain he advanced a number of familiar points. It is seldom the object for which anything has been contrived, but it is often a salutary provision. It teaches vigilance and caution, and as a monitor gives warning that something is wrong. It is seldom of long duration, and its cessation gives added pleasure. Even bodily disease is rarely fatal, and the body possesses a natural capacity for recovery. Mortal disease reconciles us to death by removing gradually or suddenly its horror. Although death brings the pain of separation, a capacity only rarely shared by animals, it seems better that we should have these affections, the source of many virtues and joys as well as of sorrows, rather than be reduced to a state of apathy and selfishness. Again Paley did not agree that the distinctions of status within society contributed greatly to happiness or unhappiness; he pointed out that cruelties and misfortunes of tyranny, rebellion, war, and other private or public misdemeanours, are all due to man's freedom. Free agency in its very essence implies liability to abuse, yet deprive man of this freedom and his nature is subverted. Moral character depends upon the possibility of going wrong and even the bad qualities of mankind have their origin in their good ones.

Yet how can we reconcile so much in the world that appears to be due to chance with the providential rule of a supreme and benevolent Will? Paley argued that there must be some chance in the midst of design; events which are not designed necessarily arise from the pursuit of events which are designed. One man travels from London to York, another from York to London. Both do so from design, yet they meet by chance, accidentally, although we can also say that it had to be. The purposes behind the journeys could be innocent or good, yet the chance meeting might have unfortunate consequences for both. At the same time it may often be that, owing to the ignorance of the observer, events will have the appearance of chance, whereas they may well proceed from intelligence and design. This is particularly true of our judgements about God's actions. We can know but little of his mind; hence many of his acts in the world appear to us mere chance. At the same time it is better that we should be uncertain concerning many events, such as the length of our human lives. If mortality followed a fixed rule, it would produce complacency in those at a distance from it, and this would result in great disorders; whereas those near to it would approach it with horror. Paley gives a definition of providence as God's creative and continuing care, but he recognized that the appearance of chance is undoubtedly the greatest problem a doctrine of ruling providence must face. How can this be reconciled with an ordered, purposive state of things? The only solution, Paley thought, is that the appearance of disorder is consistent with life regarded as a *preparatory* state. People find themselves, apparently by chance, in very varied circumstances, some favourable and pleasant, others not so. Yet every situation, health or sickness, riches or poverty, knowledge or ignorance, liberty or bondage, civilization or barbarity, can serve the formation of character. Every blessing, including the Christian religion itself, is also a responsibility. So our ultimate or most permanent happiness depends not upon our situation in this life, but upon the way we behave in the situation. Every situation tests men, and therefore the differences between them are in the last resort immaterial. The conditions in which men find themselves may appear to follow no rule or principle, but there is most correct justice in the way in which men are rewarded for the use they make of these circumstances. Even if the order of things often appears unjust, so that happiness and misery do not inevitably follow virtue and vice, this provides opportunities for the display of the virtues most acceptable to God—patience and composure under affliction and pain, a steadfast confidence in God and reliance upon his final goodness when everything is adverse; and, above all, a cordial desire for the happiness of others when we are deprived of our own. Moreover, it is better that our happiness in this life should not be too great, otherwise we should be in danger of forgetting that life here is meant to be a preparation for the future.

Paley set out his position on the basis of a natural theology, apart from revelation. Perhaps he said as much as was possible from this standpoint, and in this sense he summed up the eighteenth-century tradition. He presented a conception of providence in terms of this point of view. As we have seen, it meant for him primarily the way in which the world is ordered and sustained. The universe follows laws which are the expression of God's nature and power: if a man lives in accordance with God's design, which means a future state of happiness, and if he sets himself to live virtuously in preparation for that future, he will find that the world, as well as his own constitution, is admirably suited to the production of those moral virtues which are the prerequisite for that future state. Paley did not exclude the Christian revelation, but he believed that its greatest contribution is to lay before us grounds for expecting a future restoration of life and a day of account and retribution. This it does through Christ's resurrection, which was confirmed and established by miracles. But following that vital attestation God committed the future progress of the Christian religion "to the natural means of human communication and to the influence of those causes by which human conduct and human affairs are governed. The seed being sown, was left to vegetate; the leaven being inserted, was left to ferment; and both according to the laws of nature."[4] Paley added that these laws of nature are controlled by that providence which conducts the affairs of the universe, although we cannot generally discern that this is so. Hence the Christian religion, having come into the world, was left to act in accordance with the same laws which control the world. The case would appear to be similar to that of the individual; whilst he may not expect his life to be directed by any special intervention of providence, by trusting in God and by obedience to his commands, he can rest with confidence upon the assurance that his life is being directed by those principles which govern the world as a whole. To believe that reality *is* like this, namely, that it is governed by God's goodness, and to believe that virtue will be rewarded in the future by God's goodness, is to believe in God's providence.

Christian piety must always hold to a tension between acceptance of the world as it is and protest against it. The danger which lurks behind the type of thought we have been reviewing is a too easy-going acceptance of things as they are—what has been called cosmic toryism. Any insistence upon the general providential ordering of events is of course threatened by this, and it is instructive to find it coming to expression in one way or another in various types of eighteenth-century thought. Leibniz defended the theory that, in spite of evil, this is the best of all possible worlds. At a more popular level, the English country gentleman, Soames Jenyns, defended the *status quo* in his book *Free Enquiry into the Nature and Origin of Evil* (1757), in which he proved to his own satisfaction that "God is the author of all the natural evils in the universe, 'that is, of the fewest possible in the nature of things' ".[5] Even Paley was not averse to justifying the threefold order of ministry in the Established Church by the argument that it corresponded to the distinctions in lay society, and provided that people in the different strata of social life should have clergy suited to their own levels! It has of course been pointed out that in the early and middle years of the eighteenth century the wealthy and educated of Europe probably enjoyed the nearest approach to happiness ever experienced by man, although it must be doubted whether such judgements have any meaning. To be sure not all thinkers felt this satisfaction. Some cast doubts upon the entirely satisfactory character of nature on the one hand, others upon man's nature and the civilization he has created on the other. Examples of both attitudes can be found in the English religious scene.

---

[4] *Evidences of Christianity*, pp. 391ff.
[5] B. Willey, op. cit., p. 53.

Joseph Butler, amongst the greatest English theologians and moralists, accepted in his famous *Analogy of Religion* (1736) the familiar position that our human life is part of a larger plan of things. It is best understood as a school of discipline for producing that character which is a necessary qualification for a future state of happiness and security, but the significant point is that Butler did not find nature, any more than revelation, entirely satisfactory or unambiguous. He was much more pessimistic about it than the Deists; he saw the perplexities and irrationalities of life, and, although he came down firmly on the side of Christian orthodoxy, his strength lay in the impressive way in which he surveyed all aspects of experience, and refused to claim greater confidence about nature than the facts of life justified.

Similarly, John Wesley, for all his characteristic affinity with much in the thought of the eighteenth century, was at the same time critical of much that was typical of it.[6] He often spoke of God within the traditional framework. God is referred to as Creator or even the First Cause, who is at the same time Governor over all things. He appointed and continues to appoint everything its time and place. The Christian is happy in knowing that this Intelligent Cause is Lord of all, who allots the time, place, and the circumstances for the birth of each individual, and who as Governor is the rewarder and punisher of all men. Towards men God acts no longer as mere Sovereign, but as an impartial Judge, whose judgements, being guided by justice, imply the moral freedom of those who are judged. Without this there could be no righteous judgement. At the same time Wesley admitted that occasionally God does act towards men irresistibly as Sovereign, as when he intervenes to arrest someone in a career of sin by converting him to righteousness. Similarly, in the course of the Christian life we are often conscious of God restraining us. These are instances of God doing more than justice requires by acting mercifully.

Wesley pursued the idea of God as Effective Cause as far as he was able. God sustains all things as the inward, acting principle, the only proper agent in the universe who at the same time imparts a spark of his creativity to created spirits. Chance plays no part in the government of the world, although this goes far beyond our present understanding, whether we think of nations, families, or individuals. At this point Wesley distinguished between God's sustaining benevolence of the whole creation and

[6] Cf. John Wesley, *Works* (Jackson), VI, 313ff, 325ff, 337ff, 424ff; VII, 386ff, 409ff, 431ff; X, 361ff, 474ff; XI, 1ff. *Letters* (Standard Edition), II, 256ff, 379; IV, 7ff; VI, 339.

that "superintending providence which regards the children of men". But also among men three degrees of God's providence can be discerned. The outermost circle embraces the whole of mankind; since he is the God of all, all men share in the natural provisions of his love. The interior circle encompasses the Church of Christ. All who as Christians honour God are objects of God's nearer concern. It often appears that the prince of this world has not such full power over these as over the heathen. Within the innermost circle are contained only true Christians: it is to these in particular that our Lord says, "Even the very hairs of your head are all numbered." These experience his grace in all circumstances.

Wesley was here making a point which was crucial for him and which he recognized marked him off from many of his contemporaries. The wise men of the world, he said, acknowledge a general providence, but they know not what to make of a particular providence, of which some men talk. But providence must be particular as well as general to be worthy of the name. Because, Wesley said, he believes the Bible he cannot agree with Pope that

> He sees with equal eyes, as Lord of all.
> A hero perish, or a sparrow fall.

Nor can he follow the same poet when he asserts that

> The Universal Cause
> Acts not by partial, but by general laws.

This, Wesley commented, is a common supposition, but it is inconsistent with the whole tenor of Scripture, for if God only acts by general laws no miracle was ever worked. At the same time, Wesley went further than his typical contemporaries in recognizing the providential working out of an historical purpose which was not merely the testing of individual souls. Inanimate creation is subject to God's will and can offer no opposition; but evil spirits and evil men continually oppose God and so create "numberless irregularities". Precisely at this point the riches of God's wisdom and knowledge are shown. His design is the salvation of mankind, and this involves counteracting the wickedness and folly of men. God might do this by the exercise of irresistible power; but this would imply no wisdom at all. Instead, his wisdom is shown by saving man in such a manner that his nature is not destroyed nor his liberty taken away. Wesley thus saw the course of history as a continual conflict between the will of God and human and superhuman sin. God continually sends his spirit to renew his work, and he is even now carrying on the work of repairing whatsoever is decayed, and he will do so until the end of time. Thus in spite of his conviction that God is Sovereign Lord Wesley could never acquiesce in any view of God's providence which failed to recognize the conflicts in the historical process of events. This, together with his conviction that God interposes in the lives of men to turn them from sin to holiness, prevented Wesley from subscribing wholeheartedly to the "cosmic toryism" of his age. Although he could never doubt the providential appointments of God in the created order, he was much more concerned with what men might become through God's grace, and in this he was typical of most men of the Revival.

It is not difficult to criticize some of the more obvious weaknesses of the eighteenth-century approach. Its argument for the existence of God from the design evident in creation can of course be subjected to serious philosophical and scientific objections, yet the fact that the world of nature exhibits an impressive order and constancy cannot be overlooked, whatever truth there is in the Heisenberg principle. It can be argued that the eighteenth-century thinkers often worked within too narrow a compass to satisfy the biblical theologian, and Wesley's criticisms at this point have been noted. There are few indications that they conceived of a providence which calls men to suffer with Christ for the well-being of others, since they were on the whole dominated by an individualistic scheme of rewards and punishments, and lacked a full sense of the tragic in life. Yet, just as modern ecclesiastical historians have caused many of the popular strictures on eighteenth-century church life to be modified, so there is more to be said for the thinkers of that period than is often recognized today. They did feel the need for trying to see the Christian faith set within the bounds of a universe governed by law. They did attempt to wrestle with the problem of materialistic fatalism, the view that the universe is a vast closed system of interacting physical forces, which still lurks at the back of many people's minds today. And not only did these writers at their best appreciate that there is impressive evidence for a general providential ordering of life, or even that God does often overrule for good the sinful projects of men. They glimpsed something more. In claiming that the circumstances of life *can* always be used for good they were making an affirmation about the nature of the world and God's relationship to it. If it cannot always be said that the order of events is providential as they stand—and a generation which is aware of so many cruelties and inequalities will not easily admit this—may it not be claimed nevertheless that, for the Christian at least, this order may always by the activity of faith *become* providential? The Christian cannot and should not simply acquiesce in things as they are, but must adopt a positive and creative attitude to events and circumstances, which always hold out possibilities for good, in spite of much in them that must be accounted contrary to the Divine Will. Some such conviction must lie at the root of any Christian belief about providence, and it was implied in Luther's claim that among the qualities imparted by Christ to Christians is his Kingship. This is an insight suggested also by one of the eighteenth-century hymn-writers, a poet who was certainly aware of the deeper dimension of human suffering. In "God moves in a mysterious way his wonders to perform", William Cowper ascribed the course of events to God's providential care. Yet, as Cowper himself knew, such a providence was not immediately apparent. An attitude of trust in God must be brought to the events, since "blind unbelief is sure to err, and scan his work in vain". Here was a suggestion of another element in the understanding of the meaning of providence. Faith, which is a necessary requirement in any consideration of the subject, must mean not only an attitude of passive acceptance but also one of creative activity, which with God's help can transform evil into good.

5

PROVIDENCE IN
THE THEOLOGY OF KARL BARTH

CHARLES DUTHIE

LET me begin with a quotation from Barth's *Church Dogmatics*. It comes not from III. iii. in which he deals directly with the doctrine of providence but from IV. i., the first of the three volumes on the doctrine of reconciliation. He is speaking of what he calls the "will and plan and promise of God".

> It goes beyond, or rather it precedes His will and work as Creator. Therefore it has to be distinguished from it, as something prior, which precedes it. The ordaining of salvation for man and of man for salvation is the original and basic will of God, the ground and purpose of His will as Creator. It is not that He first wills and works the being of the world and man, and then ordains it to salvation. But God creates, preserves and overrules man for this prior end and with this prior purpose, that there may be a being distinct from Himself ordained for salvation, for perfect being, for participation in His own being, because as the One who loves in freedom He has determined to exercise redemptive grace—and that there may be an object of this, His redemptive grace, a partner to receive it (pp. 9-10).

Grace! Barth's theology has been rightly described by G. C. Berkouwer, the Dutch theologian, as a theology of the "triumph of grace". Grace, according to Barth, is God reconciling the world to himself. That reconciliation takes place, has indeed already taken place in Jesus Christ. But this Jesus Christ, who is both God and man, leads us beyond history. "In Jesus Christ", Barth tells us, "we really have to do with the first and eternal Word of God at the beginning of all things."[1] What does this mean? It means that reconciliation originates in a decision taken, a

[1] IV. i. p. 50.

decree made by God in eternity. In the freedom and fullness of his overflowing love the Triune God turned outward from himself, electing man through Jesus Christ to be his man, his servant, his partner. "I will be your God and ye shall be my people" (Jer. 7.23) is the historical form of the pledge and promise of the covenant God makes with man. In his utter faithfulness he binds himself to man in Jesus Christ and in so doing binds man to himself.

I have made a beginning with what I consider to be a representative quotation from the *Church Dogmatics* and a brief interpretative comment on it because it is important to recognize that in Barth's theology every Christian doctrine, including the doctrine of providence, is worked out in relation to, and in dependence upon, the central theme. We can confirm this and at the same time introduce our subject directly by turning to the sentence which introduces and summarizes paragraph 48, "The Doctrine of Providence, its Basis and Form", the first of the four paragraphs which make up the topic of III.iii, "The Creator and His creature".

> The doctrine of providence deals with the history of created being as such, in the sense that in every respect and in its whole span this proceeds under the fatherly care of God the Creator, whose will is done and is to be seen in His election of grace, and therefore in the history of the covenant between Himself and man, and therefore in Jesus Christ (p. 3).

Baron von Hügel was fond of saying that the God of nature is the God of grace. Barth would agree; but he would want to add that we must interpret God's relation to nature from what we know of him in redemption. If God's action in Jesus Christ shows us the character of God and if God is always true to himself, then it is in this character that he works in history.

Barth enters upon his treatment of the subject by distinguishing the concept of divine providence, the Christian belief in providence, and the Christian doctrine of providence. As to the concept, while he prefers, with post-Reformation Protestant theology, to look at providence in its relation to the doctrine of creation rather than as part of the doctrine of God, he must nevertheless go back to the eternal decree of God in order to throw light on both creation and providence. If creation has to do with the initiation, providence belongs to the execution of the decree. Creation and providence are connected with, but distinct from, each other. Providence guarantees and confirms the work of creation; but it is a continuation of creation rather than creation continued. What confronts us in both creation and providence is the Lordship of God.

Barth now moves on to describe the Christian belief in providence.

> In the belief in providence the creature understands the Creator as the One who has associated Himself with it in faithfulness and constancy as this sovereign and living Lord, to precede, accompany and follow it, preserving, co-operating and overruling in all that it does and all that happens to it (p. 14).

This belief in providence is, in the strictest sense, faith; it is not a postulate or hypothesis. Moreover, it is faith in God, not in any cosmic process. It cannot be equated with a philosophy of history. Finally, it is faith in Jesus Christ, in the God who comes to us in Christ. Barth criticizes Calvin and Protestant theology in general for failing to let Christ control the belief in providence. This failure led, he believes, to what he calls a "generally apprehensible doctrine of providence" which left the way open for "belief in history" so that a time came when the word "providence" was a "favourite one on the lips of Adolf Hitler".

Barth is thus led to consider the Christian doctrine of providence. What does it mean to say that Christ controls the Christian belief in providence? It means that the one thin line in world history that leads to him as its goal is decisive for the understanding of God's relation to all occurrences in the world. That thin line is the *Heilsgeschichte*, redemption-history, "special history" as he often calls it, which is exalted above all other history. The "supreme and proper theme" of this special history is God's faithfulness. But God's faithfulness is indivisible. He is the Lord not only of the special history but of all history. If we think with the Bible, we cannot tolerate the notion of a "free and secular creaturely occurrence" which stands in a neutral relation to *Heilsgeschichte*. As Barth sees it, creaturely occurrence is both co-ordinated with and subordinated to "the occurrence of the covenant, grace and salvation" under the Lordship of God and in the interest of his Kingdom. If it can be said provisionally that creaturely occurrence is the servant and instrument of God, the theatre in which he acts, the mirror of the covenant of grace, this does not mean that creation possesses these functions in itself. It has them only as it receives them from God. A Christian doctrine of providence must therefore look at the world from the standpoint of faith, from the knowledge of God in Christ. It will have its limits and it will avoid pretensions; but it will hold fast to the conviction that the world-ruler is none other than the living God, the God and Father of Jesus Christ, the Creator and Redeemer.

Having thus indicated the main lines along which a Christian doctrine of providence must proceed, Barth must now give specific content to the doctrine. This he proceeds to do in paragraph 49, which bears the title "God the Father as Lord of His creature". This is his summary of that paragraph.

> God fulfils His fatherly lordship over His creature by preserving, accompanying and ruling the whole course of its earthly existence. He does this as His mercy is revealed and active in the creaturely sphere in Jesus Christ, and the Lordship of His Son is thus manifested to it (p. 58).

Barth then examines in turn what he calls the divine preserving, the divine accompanying, and the divine ruling.

The divine preserving is the activity by which God maintains the creature in being, giving to it a limited place and time. It is essentially the free activity of God, but it lacks the immediacy of his original act of creation and of his self-giving in grace. God works through the created order; but it is he who works, not the order. Moreover, in preserving the creature God does not create it anew from moment to moment. He rather sustains its continuing identity. And the creature needs to be preserved. Preserved from what? From overthrow, Barth tells us, by "that which is not". We here confront Barth's rather strange teaching about the Nihil, *das Nichtige*.

> That which is not is that which God as Creator did not elect or will, that which as Creator He passed over, that which according to the account in Genesis 1.2 He set behind Him as chaos, not giving it existence or being. That which is not is that which is actual only in the negativity allotted to it by the divine decision, only in its exclusion from creation, only, if we may put it thus, at the left hand of God. But in this way it is truly actual and relevant and even active after its own particular fashion (p. 74).

Barth later devotes a long section of III.iii. to an examination of the Nihil. While it would take too long to undertake a full critical evaluation of Barth's philosophy of the Nihil, we must at least pose several pertinent questions. Can Barth really derive *das Nichtige* from Scripture? Is he not actually venturing into the philosophical speculation which he believes the theologian should avoid? Is his whole conception anything other than a piece of unconvincing mythology? Barth wants to hold that *das Nichtige* could not have come into being without the action of God in creation and at the same time to say that, as the source of evil and sin, it is the enemy of God. This comes very

near to saying—and this Barth really wants to avoid saying—
that the creation of the world carries with it the possibility,
which in due course becomes the actuality, of evil. Such a view
certainly accords with Barth's repeated assertion that God has
foreordained man to salvation. It would be unfair to leave the
subject without reminding ourselves that for Barth the struggle
with the Nihil is God's affair, not ours. God compels the Nihil
to be his servant. Through Christ the Nihil will finally be overcome.

God preserves the creature within the limits he prescribes for
it, delighting in the life of the world and especially in the sons
of men. God will preserve man not by extending his temporal
existence but by allowing him to continue eternally before him.
And here Barth breaks out into poetic vision in a passage so
unusual for him that it is worth quoting in full.

> And one day—to speak in temporal terms—when the totality of
> everything that was and is and will be will only have been, then
> in the totality of its temporal duration it will still be open and
> present to Him, and therefore preserved; eternally preserved; reveal-
> ed in all its greatness and littleness; judged according to its rightness
> or wrongness, its value or lack of value; but revealed in its partici-
> pation in the love which He Himself has directed towards it.
> Therefore nothing will escape Him; no aspect of the great game of
> creation; no moment of human life; no thinking thought; no word
> spoken; no secret or insignificant enterprise or deed or omission
> with all its interaction and effects; no suffering or joy; no sincerity
> or lie; no secret event in heaven or too well-known event on earth;
> no ray of sunlight; no note which has ever sounded; no colour
> which has ever been revealed, possibly in the darkness of oceanic
> depths where the eye of man has never perceived it; no wing-
> beat of the day-fly in far-flung epochs of geological time. Every-
> thing will be present to Him exactly as it was or is or will be,
> in all its reality, in the whole temporal course of its activity, in
> its strength or weakness, in its majesty or meanness. He will not
> allow anything to perish, but will hold it in the hollow of His
> hand as He has always done, and does, and will do. He will not be
> alone in eternity, but with the creature. He will allow it to partake
> of His own eternal life. And in this way the creature will continue
> to be, in its limitation, even in its limited temporal duration.[2]

We come next to the divine accompanying. In this phase of
the argument Barth expounds the unique relation that subsists
between the activity of God and that of the creature. God
recognizes and respects the autonomous activity of the creature;
but this activity is always accompanied and surrounded by his

[2] III. iii, pp. 89-90.

own activity. God does not act only *towards* man—man would then be an object; he acts also *with* man, man becoming then his companion. But Barth goes farther.

> He takes it (the creature) to Himself as such and in general in such sort that He co-operates with it, preceding, accompanying and following all its being and activity, so that all the activity of the creature is primarily and simultaneously and subsequently His own activity and therefore a part of the actualisation of His own will revealed and triumphant in Jesus Christ (p. 105).

In his attempt to show this mysteriously close relation between God's activity and man's, Barth has clearly enlarged the initial idea of accompanying. God's activity not only accompanies man's; it precedes and follows it. The precedence is interpreted in terms of foreordination. Calvin was not wrong in taking the idea of predestination seriously; he was wrong in failing to connect it with Christ. The accompanying is understood not simple as God acting with man but as the coincidence of divine and human action which is made possible by the fact that God and man belong to two entirely different orders. Barth leaves us in no doubt about what he means. "He would not be God at all if He were not the living God, if there were a single point where He was absent or inactive, or only partly active or restricted in His action" (p. 133). Or again "It is God who affects creaturely occurence, that is, He is the living basis of its occurrence as such, and the living basis of its order and form" (p. 132). Or even more clearly "We have to understand the activity of God and that of the creature as a single action" (p. 132), and "creaturely events take place as God Himself acts".

Why do we stumble over the faith that God is "the One who is always active in, over and with His creatures by His Word and Spirit" (p. 143)? Barth addresses himself to what he describes as an anxiety-complex about God.

> What is the value of all our thought and talk about Christ and His resurrection, about grace, about the glory of our regeneration and the new creation, about the majesty of the Word of God, about the Church as a divine institution, about the causative and cognitive powers of the sacraments, if in face of the simple demand to acknowledge God as the One who does all in all we are suddenly gripped by anxiety, as though perhaps we were ascribing too much to God and too little to the creature, as though perhaps we were encroaching too far on the particularity and autonomy of creaturely activity and especially on human freedom and responsibility? As if there could be any sense in sheltering from such a demand under the safe cover of a crude or subtle synergism!

> What sorry lip-servants we are! And there is a reason for it.
> For in the very depths of the Church, in the very depths of the
> Christian conscience and Christian theology, our fear of God is in
> fact far stronger than the love with which we are able to love
> God (p. 147).

This is a passage which makes us ask, even when we appreciate
what Barth is trying to say, whether he himself has not such an
anxiety-complex with regard to synergism that he fails to do
justice to the reality and freedom of man.

We can speak briefly of the activity of God which follows
that of the creature. "God outruns the creature", writes Barth,
"and His activity follows the activity of the creature, in the
sense that He acts as the Lord even of the effects of creaturely
activity" (p. 152). When I act, what I do passes out of my
control. It is in the hands of God and under the judgement of
God and at the disposal of God. This should lead not to resigna-
tion but to assurance and hope. God rules, and he is Father.

And so we come to the third activity of God, the divine ruling.
It is God and God alone who rules. The fact that he rules includes the further fact that he himself is the goal he appoints
for the creature. "Proceeding from God and accompanied by God,
the creature must also return to God" (p. 158). Thus "the glory
of God is the salvation and glorification of the creature" (p. 159).
The way of God in his rule cannot be calculated. God is a God of
surprises. But this does not mean that he is to be found only
in the extraordinary. If he is the God of miracle, he is also the
lover of law and order. "He loves the law-abiding bourgeois as
well as the nomad" (p. 161). Moreover, God is not to be identified
with any cosmic principle such as fate on the one side or chance
on the other. How then does he rule? Barth repeats in a new form
what he has already said in describing God's preserving and
accompanying.

> The rule of God is the operation of God over and with the temporal
> history of that reality which is distinct from God: the operation
> by which He arranges the course of that history, maintains and
> executes His own will within it, and directs it wholly and utterly
> in accordance with that will (p. 164).

Once again we stand before the mysterious coincidence of divine
and human action. "He makes the activity of the creature the
means of His own activity. He gives to the creature a part in His
own operation" (p. 165). Thus "Between the sovereignty of God
and the freedom of the creature there is no contradiction. The
freedom of its activity does not exclude but includes the fact
that it is controlled by God" (p. 166). But it does not follow

from this that God is man's oppressor. Quite the contrary. The lowliness of the creature in relation to God is its exaltation. "If it is nothing without Him, it is everything by Him; everything, that is, that He its Creator and Lord has determined and ascribed and allotted to it; everything that He will continue to be for it, and to execute with and by it" (p. 170).

It is perhaps necessary to add before continuing the exposition that while Barth keeps affirming the coincidence of divine and human action, he leaves his statements on the level of generalization and does not show how this coincidence works out in practice in daily life.

Who is this God who rules the world, Barth now asks? He is not the supreme being, as envisaged in some philosophies, but the King of Israel, in other words the God who reveals himself in redemption-history. If we are to understand world-events, we must therefore look at them from the vantage-point of the particular events attested in the Bible. Conversely we must look back from world-events to redemption-history. It does not follow, however, that we can read the rule of God clearly from world-history. God is as much hidden as revealed and we can detect only traces of his rule.

If there is an element of hiddenness about the rule of God in the world, there are not lacking certain signs for those who have eyes to see and ears to hear. Barth draws attention to four of these signs. The first is the history of holy Scripture. Its origin, its transmission, its interpretation and its influence constitute a remarkable witness to God. The second is the history of the Church. Despite its weaknesses and follies the Church has shown an uncanny power of resistance and of renewal. Let Barth speak in his own words.

> Certainly, if we are members of the Church participating for ourselves in its daily renewal we learn to be amazed at the economy which rules in its history, not merely modulating and correcting but constantly reviving, so that it seems to be ordained that a secularised Christianity should always be followed by the counter-thrust of a vigorously eschatological, a narrow and restricted by that of an open and free, an old-fashioned by that of a modern, an intellectualised by that of a practical, a naive by that of an instructed, an indolent by that of an active, an over-busy by that of a contemplative, a clerical by that of a lay, and a too popular by that of a healthy authoritarian. These have all been actual renewals. They have not been accomplished without new errors and apostasy, but from the standpoint of the basis of the Church they still have to be recognised as necessary renewals, in which the Church as a whole has come to life again, in which we

can on the whole, therefore, recognise a guiding of the Church,
a guiding which does not ever desire its death, but always its life.
And if we do not fail to see this, we shall not fail to see a trace
of the divine world-governance in the Church which is also a trace
of the divine world-governance as such (p. 210).

The third sign is the astonishing history of the Jews. That this
race has persisted despite dispersion and persecution is a cause
for wonder. It cannot be separated from the fact of God's election.
"It costs something to be the chosen people", Barth says, "and the
Jews are paying the price" (p. 220). Providence has arranged it
that the Jews will survive even the most virulent anti-Semitism.
Their presence in the world is a reminder, first, that we are all
involved with them in a revolt against God, and, second, that with
the Jewish people God has elected all peoples. Barth's fourth and
final sign is what he calls the limitation of life. We are born, we
live for a certain time, and then we die. To the eye of faith man's
beginning and end "reflect two great acts of God at the beginning
and end of all things, the creation and the consummation" (p. 230).
They point to two different acts of God's lordship, his giving and
his taking. And so "in our movement from birth to death we are
the sign and testimony to ourselves of this Lord of life and
death, of the lordship of this God" (p. 235).

Paragraph 49, with which we are chiefly concerned, concludes
with a long section entitled "The Christian under the Universal
Lordship of God the Father". While all men are under the universal lordship of God the Christian is the man who recognizes
this and affirms it. Through no merit of his own he sees what
others do not see. He has therefore "a true knowledge of the providence and universal lordship of God" (p. 242). This does not mean
that he is never bewildered by the riddles of the world-process.
He often is. He asks the questions that others ask. He knows that
there are no master-keys of man's devising which can unlock
every mystery. Barth thus describes him.

> He is the one man who will always be the most surprised, the most
> affected, the most apprehensive and the most joyful in the face of
> events. He will not be like an ant which has foreseen everything
> in advance, but like a child in a forest, or on Christmas Eve; one
> who is always rightly astonished by events, by the encounters and
> experiences which overtake him, and the cares and duties laid
> upon him. He is the one who is constantly forced to begin afresh,
> wrestling with the possibilities which open out to him and the
> impossibilities which oppose him. If we may put it in this way,
> life in the world, with all its joys and sorrows and contemplation
> and activity, will always be for him a really interesting matter,

or, to use a bolder expression, it will be an adventure, for which he for his part has ultimately and basically no qualifications of his own (p. 243).

In this adventure the Christian's knowledge of providence and of God's lordship is rooted in the Christian life and dependent at every point on that life. It is from within the interrelated activities of faith, obedience, and prayer—and Barth's commentary on all three is illuminating and helpful—that God's action in the world is truly understood. The subjective element in faith, obedience, and prayer must be affirmed—it is our faith, our obedience, our prayer; but Barth would not be Barth did he not conclude the argument of this long paragraph by telling us that the subjective element "conceals and contains and actualises the most objective of all things, the Lordship of One who as King of Israel and King of the Kingdom of grace holds all things in His own hands, and directs everything that occurs in this world for the best: per Jesum Christum, Dominum nostrum" (p. 288).

I have confined myself, in the main, to expounding what Barth says in the first half of III. iii., because it is necessary to allow Barth to speak for himself before venturing to assess the value of what he says. I have made no reference to his lengthy discussion of angels and demons and touched but lightly on his difficult notion of the Nihil. These themes demand a fuller consideration than is here possible. But even without such consideration we are now in a position to offer some comment upon the main outline of his teaching on providence.

It is a striking fact, and one not always fully appreciated by those who differ from him, that, although Barth goes his own distinctive way, he does not do so without weighing the opinions of those who have a title to be heard on the theme under discussion. Thus Augustine, Luther, Calvin, post-Reformation Protestant theology come under careful scrutiny and appraisal— but also Aquinas, Leibniz, Nietzche, Sartre, and many others. Again and again Barth shows himself to be a generous receiver and an acute critic. Although his repetitiveness is often wearisome, his thought is at times fresh and subtle and deep, opening new paths for serious theology.

What cannot fail to impress the reader who has the strength and patience to follow the course of Barth's reflection on the doctrine of providence is precisely what impresses wherever the *Church Dogmatics* is opened: here is a man who takes God with the utmost seriousness, which does not mean without great joy. It is something in our new age of doubt to have a theologian who speaks forthrightly and confidently about God and the activity of

God. A good deal has been said in recent years in favour of Tillich's criticism that traditional theology has made God the greatest of all beings instead of the true ultimate "in whom we live and move and have our being". It must be said of Barth, however, that he has made a very strenuous effort to construe God as truly ultimate in his teaching on the lordship of God. It is his sense of the absolute lordship of God that makes him reluctant to employ the concept of "cause" when dealing with God's activity and his relation to natural or creaturely happenings lest God and his freedom be made subordinate and subservient to "causality". This lordship is universal. "He would not be God at all if he were not the living God, if there were a single point where He was absent or inactive or only partly active or restricted in His action" (p. 133). But this lordship must be rightly understood. It is the lordship of the God and Father of Jesus Christ. We can ascribe to God no other character than that which is derived from his self-disclosure in his Son.

We may be grateful to Barth for reminding us so forcefully that the world is God's and that he is a God who cares and has the power to bring his purpose to fulfilment. But what are we to make of his central contention about the coincidence of divine and human action? The following statements are characteristic. "We have to understand the activity of God and that of the creature as a single action" (p. 113). "God neither adds nor subtracts in relation to the activity of the creature" (p. 136). God is "the One who is always active in, with and over His creatures by His Word and Spirit" (p. 143). We have a right to ask whence Barth derives these naked assertions. It would be difficult to make the claim that they are all derived from the Bible, even if it were by a process of inference or interpretation. Some might possibly be derived from the experience of Christian faith; but this is a source which always has an ambiguous status in Barth's eyes. They look much more, even to the sympathetic observer, like an expression of Barth's own philosophy. Convinced of the all-embracing lordship of God and compelled to recognize the reality of human actions within the same world he simply puts the two things together and affirms their unity while holding fast to the transcendent character of the activity of God. The junction between God's action and man's is mysterious and unfathomable. What else can we expect if God be God?

It may be, of course, that, unless we capitulate to the notion of a finite God, and even if we find Barth's own statements unsatisfactory, we have to acknowledge that Barth is pointing us in the right direction when he affirms the element of mystery and transcendence in the presence of God to our action. Christian thinkers of a very different stamp have come to a not dissimilar conclusion. I cite, for example, A. M. Farrer in his most recent books *A Science of God?* (1966) and *Faith and Speculation* (1967). He writes in the latter "God's agency must actually be such as to work omnipotently on, in or through creaturely agencies without either forcing them or competing with them" (p. 62). When he comes to examine what he calls the "causal joint" between God's action and man's, Farrer, like Barth, has to confess ignorance in face of mystery. "Both the divine and the human actions remain real and therefore free in the union between them; not knowing the modality of the divine action we cannot pose the problem of their mutual relation" (p. 66). He is no more disposed than Barth to have recourse to the idea of God as *anima mundi*. "God can be the Universal Mind only by transcending that multiplicity which the Universe is" (p. 175). If his metaphysical and apologetic interest marks him off from Barth, his coming to rest in a theology of God as effective and unconditioned will bring him very near indeed.

To acknowledge that Barth may be pointing us in the right direction does not commit us to accepting the general framework of his thought. There are many points at which he must be challenged. One of these is his understanding of human nature. In his endeavour to do justice to the lordship of God, does he do less than justice to human freedom and activity? Barth, you will recall, chided Christians for the unworthy anxiety that too much might be ascribed to God. But despite his growing readiness to affirm the reality of man—because God affirms it—does he himself not betray an equally unworthy anxiety lest one excessive word about man should dishonour God? Here we face the issue that meets us in almost every aspect of Barth's theological system. The crux is found in the doctrine of reconciliation. Granted that there is a danger of falling into synergism, of thinking that man is the co-saviour of himself along with God, must we not take full measure of the fact that, although man is not the author of his own salvation, he is involved as a person in that salvation, responding as well as receiving, indeed responding in so far as he does receive? In his book *The Theology of Karl Barth: an Introduction* (1964), Dr Hartwell, after expounding Barth with knowledge and sympathy can nevertheless write:

> The proposition that man's acknowledgement and acceptance of God's grace in Jesus Christ is man's own free and responsible decision and action implies, contrary to Barth's teaching, a co-operation of some sort on the part of man. In his legitimate

endeavour to make quite clear that in the relationship between God and man God works everything and man can add nothing to it, Barth goes too far in denying any co-operation on man's part (p. 186).

In making this criticism Dr Hartwell still concedes to Barth that this co-operation on man's part is the work of God's grace. It is possible to do this, however, and still to think that Barth has failed to do justice to the human element in the "paradox of grace", the "I yet not I but Christ". If faith is both the gift of God and my free act, then, as H. R. Mackintosh used to urge, we must guard against the one-sided interpretation for which faith is nothing more than the Holy Spirit bending back upon himself *through me*.

Barth is always concerned to uphold the honour of God and believes that if it is not maintained there will be no honouring of man. "The honour of man is the reflection of God's own glory falling on him. Without God's honour there is no honour for man, no human worth or dignity. But the honour of God, and therefore the origin and true home of all human honour is the One in whom He has created all things and reconciled them to Himself."[3] That is a word the Church certainly needs to hear; but this word can be heard and accepted without adopting Barth's teaching on man. It is indeed true that "God does not need the creature but the creature has absolute need of God";[4] but it is also true that God respects the being of those whom he has created in his own image. Barth does not take proper acount of what may be called the tensional because truly personal relationship between God and man. It is a relationship which by its very nature gives to man the opportunity either to co-operate or to resist. He can say yes or he can say no to God.

Any attempt to state a Christian view of providence must take account not only of God's relation to man but of God's relation to events in the natural world. Indeed, God, man, and natural occurrences require to be viewed together. Here we must confess that, although Barth has often illuminating things to say, he is in the end disappointing. Just as he fails to grant the human person its proper freedom (although he has much to say of man as chosen by God to be his "dear partner"), so he fails to give the world what H. H. Farmer calls its "relative independence". It is hardly satisfactory to speak of the world as God's good creation, on the one hand, and then, on the other, as a world affected by the Nihil. It would surely be

---

[3] III. iv, p. 685.
[4] III. iii, p. 108.

better, with de Chardin and other modern writers, to accept the universe as a universe in which evil arises through the processes of disorder and failure, of decay, of solitude and anxiety, and of growth itself. Evil comes to be precisely because our world is a world built for the development of freedom, the growth in wisdom and love of personal spirits. Barth seems to be haunted by the fear of making God "the author of evil". The Nihil might even be regarded as a device to avoid this possibility. But what if God accepts the responsibility for creating a world in which evil is first a possibility and then a reality? To maintain this is not creaturely impertinence or irreverence, for we know that God has involved himself at great cost in the life, death, and resurrection of Jesus Christ. This is the measure of his acceptance of responsibility for giving man life and freedom. Barth has led us a certain distance along this path by his unwearied insistence on God's faithfulness in the covenant-love in which he binds himself to his people and in so doing binds his people to himself. While the development of the idea of a divine involvement is not without dangers, the idea itself opens the way to a more dynamic view of history and of the world than we find in Barth. God can be involved without losing his lordship, that transcendence which Barth values so highly and which is often under attack in some modern theologies. Barth's theology and his understanding of providence could profit from that element of venture which we find, however imperfectly expressed, in the thought of Whitehead and de Chardin and which is surely in a measure of accord with the biblical faith in the "living God".

It has often been said that the reader who takes Barth seriously is likely either to succumb to his way of thinking or to reject it utterly. This is a false alternative. It is possible to learn from Barth without wholly agreeing with him. When we examine his treatment of the idea of providence, we find it disappointing because it does not correspond to what we take to be reasoned and reasonable Christian apologetic. We find it too often to be full of confident assertions which are not properly grounded. We do not see much in it that throws light on the vexing problem of "the absence of God". We are sometimes left with the unhappy impression that the truth which Barth is expounding is left suspended in the air, unrelated to the life which we live on earth. A dozen different criticisms, all of them with point, can be levelled against his theology of providence. What, then, if anything, is there of value that remains?

I should single out first the perhaps obvious but fundamental principle that a Christian view of providence can only be constructed from within the circle of Christian faith. We think and speak as believers. Faith is not sight and can continue and even flourish in the face of perplexities because it lives by being directed to the object of faith, which is God himself. In the second place, this God to whom faith looks is not any God and certainly not a God whose nature is deduced from our experience of the world or by metaphysical thought; he is the God who has made himself known in Jesus Christ. It is urgently necessary to cling to this insight when discussing God's relation to the world. The character of God and the action that springs from that character can only too easily be coloured by notions that are not derived from, and are incompatible with, the self-disclosure of God in Christ—to the point, indeed, where God almost loses his personal character. Finally, and despite the criticisms we have already brought against Barth's understanding of the coincidence of divine and human action, there is worth in Barth's endeavour to combine the universal lordship of God over and in all "creaturely occurrences" with the idea of God's transcendence. We must be prepared to give meaning to the phrase "the rule of God". It has biblical warrant.

The God who rules despite man's sin and who has the power to fulfil his good purpose is always for Barth the God of "grace". And grace is sovereign because God is. What is needed to correct and to amplify Barth's teaching is the reminder that once we have seen God in Jesus we know that this grace is not only condescending and undeserved, it is persuasive and accommodating. Because he is Love, God lays himself alongside his world and the personal beings he has created. He seeks to win without dominating. The application of this idea to Barth's theology as a whole would compel some modification not only in his teaching on providence but on much else.

6

PROVIDENCE AND SCIENCE

HUW OWEN

THE idea of providence has four main aspects. It indicates firstly that God foresees future events, secondly that he controls them, thirdly that he cares for his creatures, and fourthly that he is working out a purpose in them. Inevitably these aspects overlap; but it is convenient to treat them separately. My aim is to discover the impact (if any) of science—by which I mean the *natural* sciences—on them.

Obviously the first aspect—God's foresight—lies wholly outside the province of science. The questions that arise here are purely metaphysical. The two most pressing are these. Does God actually foreknow events or know them timelessly within the *totum simul* of his pure actuality? If he does foreknow them, does he foreknow all or only some of them (for example, those that do not depend on free will)? If these questions are answerable by the human mind, the answers are not influenced by any scientific theory or datum.

Secondly, God's providence means his "control" of the world that he created. How, then, does he exercise this control? The general answer that Christians give to this question is that he controls it partly through the regularity of nature, and partly through the response of human minds to their environment. Our grounds for giving this answer (like all our grounds for faith) are non-scientific. They consist in the usual triad: reason, revelation, and experience. Yet science impinges on faith here in many ways of which I have chosen three. A consideration of these constitutes the bulk of my paper.

The first point I shall consider takes the form of a *prima facie* incompatibility between science and a divine Controller. One of the main land-marks in science during this century has been the advent of quantum physics in general and Heisenberg's

77

"Uncertainty Principle" or "Principle of Indeterminacy" in particular. According to this principle nature, at the atomic level, does not behave according to laws which permit exact prediction. At this level (as Ian Barbour puts it in his useful survey), "Laplace's claim that all future events could be predicted from knowledge of the present is abandoned; for we cannot predict both exact position and exact velocity, and we can calculate only probabilities for the future."[1]

Now, it might be said that the presence of a random element (or, conversely, the absence of absolute determination) at the root of nature is incompatible with belief in an omnipotent Designer. In reply I would make the following two points.

First (as Barbour proceeds to state), it is not established that Heisenberg's principle signifies an objective and irreducible element of randomness in nature. Two other possibilities remain. One can hold that the limitations of the human mind prevent us from ever knowing whether atomic activity is or is not ultimately indeterminate. Or one can hold (with Einstein) that it is ultimately determinate, but that its causal laws have not yet been discovered. Here is a clear application of the important maxim that where scientists differ on scientific matters it is inappropriate for theologians to dogmatize.

Secondly, even if there is an objective and irreducible element of randomness at the atomic level, the regularity of nature at the macro-level of observable objects remains; and the latter level is the one that concerns us as subjects of personal activity. Thus, even if the electrons that compose a flame move in a random way, the flame is always hot, it will always cook my food, it will always burn my hand if I am foolish enough to test its power. That is a point to which I shall return in another context.

It therefore seems to me that, even if there is an ultimate indeterminacy in the sub-observable constituents of matter, theists need not be disturbed; for such an indeterminacy is overcome at the only level that concerns man's conscious life. And I cannot see any grounds for regarding such indeterminacy *in itself* as either specially congruous or specially incongruous with belief in a designing Mind. Why should not God permit a limited degree of indeterminacy in nature, as he has permitted it in persons (as a condition of their moral choice)?

There is, however, another aspect of this question which is more serious. This concerns the element of "chance" which, according to Darwinians, operates in the course of evolution. Species (they tell us) evolve by a series of fortuitous variations or (to use the

[1] *Issues in Science and Religion* (1966), p. 298.

later word) mutations. It is important to realize that this is quite a different case from the case of quantum physics. In this case we are attributing to chance the very existence of species (including our own); but in the case of quantum physics we are dealing merely with the behaviour of an already existing form of in-organic matter. Again, the behaviour of micro-particles con-forms to empirically established laws of probability which enable them to constitute the world of macro-entities; but the emergence of organisms by pure chance is so vastly improbable as to be inconceivable. This improbability is in fact one of the strongest purely rational grounds for postulating a directing Intelligence. And so I come to my second point.

The second point at which science impinges on providence is the celebrated argument from design. Although this argument is often held in disrepute today, we must remember that it is not only the most popular but also one which, to some extent and in some form, has won the assent of the greatest philosophers (notably Aquinas and Kant). The basis of it is that some, if not all, aspects of nature cannot be explained (at any rate fully) unless we suppose that they are directed by a cosmic Mind which possesses at least some of the properties of the Christian God.

The argument is often disparaged today on the ground that scientific explanations have filled those gaps in our knowledge into which a theistic explanation was previously inserted. It is thought that where we once saw a need for postulating a final cause (that is, some kind of directing Mind) we can now be content with efficient causes (that is, those conditions specified by empirical investigation). On this view the theistic explanation is otiose.

However, two things must be said at once. First, there may be "gaps" left by scientific explanation which by their very nature cannot be filled except by some kind of metaphysical explanation. Obviously it is both logically invalid and religiously hazardous to use "God" as a substitute for a purely scientific explanation which is not now available but which may one day come to light. Yet there may be facts which in principle cannot be explained scientifically but which can be explained meta-physically. Secondly, philosophers whose scientific knowledge and powers of reflection are indisputable continue to hold that a teleological explanation of nature is required. The most impressive example know to me is Errol Harris's *The Foundations of Meta-physics in Science* (1965). On the basis of immense technical information, Harris concludes that nature exhibits a "nisus" to-wards "wholeness", and that it demands a teleological explanation in terms of an "organizing principle". But what is this principle? Having rejected (rightly, as I believe) Driesch's "entelechies", Bergson's *élan vital*, and Whitehead's "appetition", Harris is left only with the Christian God (or a being closely resembling him).

It seems to me that science sometimes strengthens the teleological argument, and that it never weakens it. The fundamental point is the order of the universe. This remains as impressive as ever. Even if there is an objectively indeterminable element in the atomic world, the latter is nevertheless governed by statistical laws of probability, and it nevertheless forms the basis of the fixed, regular, and predictable world of macro-objects. How, then, are we to account for this massive, persistent, and interlocking order?

It has been objected that, since the world is bound to possess some kind of order, there is nothing surprising in the particular order that it does in fact possess. But a disordered universe is conceivable. It would be a universe in which (as H. D. Lewis puts it in his answer to T. Macpherson's statement of this objection) "flames would be hot one moment, cold another, water would freeze in the fire and melt there next time, nothing would retain its weight or solidity but vary and fluctuate beyond the wildest of delirious dreams".[2]

Unless we postulate a directing Mind we must account for the world's order by either "chance" or "necessity". The postulation of chance is not logically impossible; but the constantly increasing odds against it are so enormous that the acceptance of it is profoundly irrational. The odds against the universe achieving its present order even once are enormous; the odds against it *maintaining* this order (either with or without a random base) are inconceivable. Here is a recent statement of the point.

> To invoke chance, even in a relative sense, to explain the order of the world is to invoke what would be rejected in every other department of life and investigation. When four bridge-players each get a complete suit of cards, they write to papers about it. If a bridge-player invariably dealt himself a complete suit of trump cards he would not be called a lucky man.[3]

A. C. Ewing uses the same simile to make the same point in an article in the first number of *Religious Studies*.[4]

The only non-theistic alternative to chance is necessity. The universe (it may be claimed) *must* possess its order. This claim is untenable. Since everything is contingent its properties must also

[2] *Philosophy of Religion* (1965), p. 185.
[3] T. Gornall, *A Philosophy of God* (1962), p. 204.
[4] October 1965, p. 40.

be contingent. It is self-contradictory to say that x's essence is necessary although its existence is contingent; for, although essence and existence are notionally distinguishable, they are ontologically inseparable. Hence all things might be different from what they are. In fact they are orderly and intelligible; but they might have been (and at this very moment might become) chaotic in one of innumerable ways.

Yet (it may be said) we assume natural necessity in at least one sphere: causation. To this there are two replies. First, scientists seem able to dispense with the idea of causal necessity; so that we cannot expect support for the idea from them. Secondly, even if such necessity exists, it is wholly contingent; so that statements of it are wholly conditional. The most that any causal law can state is that *if* x retains its properties (including its causal ones), and *if* conditions *abc* hold, y must follow. We cannot remove the "ifs". Causal laws are our abstractions from the patterned energy of nature; but at any time, just as the energy could disappear, so also could the pattern.

This argument applies to the total order of the world throughout its history; it is universal in its scope; and so it is logically sufficient. But I believe that it has a special application to the theory (which is also the scientifically established fact) of evolution. The question is whether "chance variation" and "natural selection" are sufficient to account for the data. I do not believe that they are for the following reasons:

1. The degree of complexity involved in the evolution of many organisms is so great that an explanation in terms of random change is rationally unacceptable. The classical case remains the formation of the eye. The number of successive modifications involved in the construction of this astonishingly complex organ made Darwin "shudder". The vast improbability that these modifications would have taken place by "chance" is (to quote Harris) "quite as impressive as Bergson maintained".[5]

2. The phrase "natural selection" is grossly misleading in so far as it suggests a personified "Nature" who picks out suitable types for survival. All the phrase can mean is, banally and negatively, that those species which cannot survive in their environment perish. It does not explain how favourable mutations persist, or how organisms are able to adapt themselves to their environment in those remarkable ways that biologists describe.

[5] Op. cit., p. 236.

6

3. Each stage in the course of evolution represents an element of novelty which is genuinely creative, and which therefore cannot be fully explained in terms of its antecedent stage. Here I wholly agree with H.W.B. Joseph's criticism of Julian Huxley in his Herbert Spencer Lecture.[6] Joseph quotes Huxley for the following statement. "New combinations and properties thus arise in time. Bergson miscalls such evolution 'creative'. We had better, with Lloyd Morgan, call it 'emergent'." To this Joseph rightly replies thus:

> Why "better", unless "emergent" means something different from "creative"? Let us consider then the common uses of the word "emerge". A chick emerges from the egg, but not till it is fully formed; Athene emerged full-armed from the head of Zeus. But does an oak thus emerge from an acorn? or a chick from a fertilized egg-cell? If the properties are really new, why not allow that they are created? Any man of science naturally boggles at the word "creative", because no change to which it can be applied is fully amenable to scientific explanation. But neither, I believe, is any process to which we can properly apply the terms "development" and "evolution".[7]

The clearest case—and the only one which I wish to put forward as conclusive—is the emergence of mind (even in the most rudimentary form of sentience) from its pre-mental, purely material, matrix. Following many distinguished philosophers (such as G. F. Stout, A. E. Taylor, and W. R. Matthews) I fail to see how this fact can be non-theistically explained without either reducing mind to matter or resorting to a form of gratuitous pan-psychism. Furthermore, the development of mental life itself from the simplest sentient organism to *homo sapiens* involves a genuine element of creativity at each stage.

If, then, chance and natural selection are not sufficient as explanatory postulates, can we be content with Harris's "nisus" towards "wholeness" and "integration"? We cannot be content with it for an obvious and conclusive reason. "Nisus" means "striving". Yet how can unconscious nature "strive" towards an "end"? This is a fatal weakness in Aristotle's teleology. And the weakness can be remedied only by theism.

Let us take as a final example a theory which purports to explain organic activity as it at present exists. This is the theory that the growth of cells is "guided" by the "coding-mechanism" of the D.N.A. molecule. Now, according to the arguments I have

[6] *The Concept of Evolution*, reprinted in his *Essays in Ancient and Modern Philosophy* (1935).
[7] Op. cit., pp. 311-12.

advanced, one would urge that an explanation of this mechanism in terms of pure chance is incredible (for how could mere acids have "hit on"—and, if "hit on", maintained—such a wonderfully complex process?). How could it have been thus "programmed" without a "programmer"? An explanation in terms of "nisus" is equally incredible; for (to quote from Aquinas's Fifth Way) "nothing that lacks awareness tends to a goal, except under the direction of someone with awareness and understanding".

This example further shows that the need for a final cause is not in the least diminished by the discovery of efficient causes (or conditions). The so-called "conflict" between efficient causes and final ones is non-existent. The more we explain nature in terms of governing principles intrinsic to it (for instance, biochemical laws) the more marvellous, and so the more enigmatic, it becomes. The theist has no need to rejoice in scientific ignorance. On the contrary, the more scientific explanations we have, the stronger the argument for divine design becomes.

The question, then, is how we are to explain the order and development in nature that scientific investigation reveals. There can be no doubt concerning the validity of this question. It is logically proper in so far as nature is not a self-existent reality which, because it is self-existent, is self-explanatory. It is rationally inevitable in so far as it completes the quest for intelligibility in natural phenomena; lastly, it has the most reputable non-logical anchorage in the wonderment that some of the finest scientific minds have felt in the presence of the data they investigate. The question, therefore, is certainly valid. It is certain too that there is no satisfactory answer except in terms of a transcendent, creative, and directing Mind.

However, does the argument imply that this Mind (*a*) not merely imparted order to the world at some first moment of time, but also preserves it by his immanent power, and (*b*) is the Creator of the world *ex nihilo*? It certainly implies (*a*). According to the basic form of the argument God's act is required for the preservation of the world's order at every moment. Furthermore, if God's creative act must be postulated for mind's emergence from matter originally in the course of evolution, it must be postulated for mind's emergence in every case throughout the world's history. Admittedly the teleological argument does not absolutely require (as the cosmological argument requires) the postulation of God as one who creates the world *ex nihilo*; but it is scarcely credible that a God who exercises such extensive control over matter did not also create it in its entirety.

I must now deal with a problem that is specially acute for the

Christian form of theism. If nature is characterized by the regularity that science both presupposes and confirms, how can God intervene in it (either miraculously or non-miraculously, and either in answer to prayer or of his own unsolicited power)? I am not going to discuss miracles, partly because to do so adequately would need another paper, but mainly because "providence" is usually taken to signify God's *normal* operations in nature.

It has been maintained that God can act in ways which, though non-miraculous, are exceptions to the normal course of nature, and are specially "providential". Thus is has been assumed that (either in response to prayer or of his own good will) God can so change natural events that rain which would otherwise not come will appear, or that a cure of an otherwise fatal illness will be effected.

I find it impossible to conceive how such a non-miraculous intervention in nature could occur. It seems to me clear (as it seemed to C. S. Lewis in an appendix to his *Miracles*) that natural events are either miraculous or non-miraculous. At any rate, there is only one way known to me of attempting to square belief in a special (non-miraculous) class of natural events with the scientific assumption of nature's macro-regularity. This way is proposed by W. G. Pollard;[8] but I find it unconvincing. Pollard suggests that the element of chance in atomic nature permits God to choose providentially (but non-miraculously) between several possibilities. This suggestion is exposed to two criticisms. First, Pollard himself admits that microcosmic "chance" becomes macrocosmic necessity. Thus he says, with reference to the solar system and the phenomena associated with it, that "there are some cases of natural phenomena in which the typical situation of alternatives governed by probabilities goes over into the special case of a single alternative in which only one thing can happen" (p. 75). Secondly, Pollard stands in danger of committing the "God of the gaps" fallacy; for, if statistical probability is one day succeeded by causal laws in micro-physics, there will be no scope for God's non-miraculous interference. In any case Pollard contradicts himself. On the one hand he suggests that a throw of dice (being an example of "chance") offers scope for a special act of providence (pp. 90-7). On the other hand he asserts that, if we knew all the physical circumstances, we could predict with certainty which way the dice would fall (pp. 41-2).

It may be said that there is one sphere of physical reality in which a "special", but non-miraculous, providence can operate —*healing*. Cannot God stimulate a sick person's recuperative

8 *Chance and Providence* (1959).

powers by an *ad hoc* action (either in answer to prayer or by his uninvited mercy)? While it would be unwise to dogmatize, I suggest the following grounds for scepticism:

1. The range within which such providential acts can be expected to operate is very narrow. We do not—and (so far as I can see) cannot—expect them in cases which fall within the scope of predictability. Who asks for a "special providence" to ensure the maintenance of his (vastly intricate) nervous system? Or—to take cases of sickness—who asks for such a providence to ensure the effects of insulin or to create resistance against arteriosclerosis?

2. As the range of medical predictability increases, the "gaps" diminish. God's "providence" will await the approval, not of the theologian, but of the doctor. And doctors (understandably) disagree in prognosis, as in diagnosis. So we shall never know with certainty whether prayer *can* avail non-miraculously.

3. We cannot have it both ways. Either we do, or we do not, see God's wisdom in causal laws and the predictions they make possible. No prayer could have availed to avert the thalidomide tragedy by a non-miraculous, "special", providence. But more extensive experiment *might* have averted it by predicting its bye-effects. I cannot imagine that any Christian would wish for the absence of strict predictability in this instance. Is it, then, reasonable for him to wish for its absence in other instances (for example, a threatening thrombosis)?

Admittedly, there is not the same difficulty in assuming God's specially "providential" action upon the *mind* of the patient in answer to prayer; for all God's acts towards and in the mind are unique. But the physical possibilities of such action are small. Thus the signatories of the Anglican Report on *The Church's Ministry of Healing* (1958), in spite of their stress on man's psychosomatic unity, conclude (rightly) that "although the state of mind can influence the course of disease, this influence is certainly restricted and in many conditions it does not operate at all for practical purposes" (p. 12).

I conclude that we cannot meaningfully speak of, or therefore pray for, specially providential but non-miraculous events of a purely physical (or material) kind. Yet this conclusion is entirely in accordance with what we know independently concerning God, his relationship to the world, and the true nature of prayer. Moreover, we can still speak of a non-miraculous event as being specially providential in the sense that, although it falls within the normal and predictable sequences of nature, it is a means whereby the believer becomes specially aware of, and responsive to, God's personal reality.

To sum up, where science is relevant, it is fully compatible with belief in (and in my view demands the postulation of) God's ceaseless direction of nature. But is science relevant to the third and fourth elements in the idea of providence—to the beliefs that God cares for his creatures and that he has a purpose for them? It has some, but not a decisive, relevance to both beliefs.

With regard to the first of these beliefs, it is obvious that, if we look at nature, we can see apparent evidence both for and against the claim that God is love. Science doubtless adds some new data on both sides; but it does not tilt the scales. While it reveals unsuspected beauty in crystals, it also reveals the life-cycle of the malaria parasite. While it gives us deeper knowledge of the wonderful ways in which our bodies are contrived and adapted to their spiritual superstructure, it also informs us that our species survived from a nature "red in tooth and claw". If we solve the problem that these conflicting data raise, we shall do so on non-scientific grounds.

With regard to the possibility of a divine purpose, the scientific investigation of past and present facts makes two complementary contributions. On the one hand it shows that man is the end towards which terrestrial evolution tends. On the other hand it rescues us from an unduly anthropocentric attitude by focusing our minds on the autonomy of sub-human organisms and disclosing, increasingly, the vastness of the universe. Yet concerning the true nature and final destiny of man it can tell us nothing. It cannot predict how man will behave (whether, for example, he will destroy himself by the power that it places in his hands). Nor can it tell him how he *ought* to behave; for the attempt to base ethics on biological evolution has proved (inevitably) to be a failure. It is not certain that science can predict even the physical fate of our species; for (as Stephen Toulmin has recently pointed out)[9] the second law of thermodynamics does not necessarily apply to the universe as a whole. Yet, even if science could predict the extinction of life (or at least human life) on this planet, such a prediction could be assimilated by Christian eschatology.

There is one last point on which I must comment. I have been considering scientific theory. However, popular attitudes are shaped to a much larger extent by the practical application of scientific theories. It may well be that the spectacular success of the applied sciences and technology has weakened a "real", if not a "notional", assent to divine providence. As *we* control more and more, God

[9] In *Metaphysical Beliefs* (1957).

(it may be assumed) controls less and less; and so (to use a current phrase) he is "edged out" of the universe. Yet, however deeply this assumption may be ingrained psychologically, it is logically false on three grounds. First, God (as First Cause) always operates through secondary causes; secondly, the latter always consist in the interaction of man's mental powers with physical nature; and, thirdly, man can control nature only in accordance with those principles with which God has endowed it.

From this discussion (which, of course, could be continued in much greater depth) I conclude that science confirms belief in God as a controlling Mind that sets the physical stage for the human drama. But concerning the drama itself and any specific divine intervention in it science has nothing to say. Hence I can bring you only to the threshold of *Geschichte* and, *a fortiori*, *Heilsgeschichte*.

7

TOWARDS A CHRISTIAN DOCTRINE
OF PROVIDENCE

SYDNEY EVANS

THIS title which I have been given makes an assumption. It takes for granted that there can be or ought to be a Christian doctrine of providence towards which a writer can direct his readers' attention. This assumption implies another, namely that woven into the way things really are in our human experience there is a strand for which the word "providence" is an appropriate pointer or "model", and about which therefore Christians can be expected to have reached or to be capable of reaching a "doctrine".

These assumptions must be investigated first. They are not self-evidently true. Some forms of the doctrine of providence we have been hearing about have led to curious interpretations of the human situation. May there not be something wrong with the underlying assumptions on the basis of which these doctrines have been formulated? To take an example from literature: the following conversation between Pastor Manders and Mrs Alving in Ibsen's *Ghosts*[1] indicates the extremes of superstition and cynicism to which a certain type of teaching about providence can give rise. The issue is whether or not the new orphanage should be insured.

MANDERS
    . . . But there's just one other thing I've been meaning to ask you several times.

MRS ALVING
    And what is that?

MANDERS
    Are the Orphanage buildings to be insured or not?

MRS ALVING
    Yes, of course they must be insured.

[1] *The Oxford Ibsen*, Vol. V (1961), pp. 361-3.

MANDERS

Ah, but wait a moment Mrs Alving. Let's examine this matter more closely.

MRS ALVING

I keep everything insured—the buildings, the contents, the crops and the stock.

MANDERS

Naturally. On your own property. I do the same . . . of course. But this is quite a different thing, you see. The Orphanage is, as it were, to be dedicated to a higher purpose.

MRS ALVING

Yes, but . . .

MANDERS

As for me personally, I don't honestly see anything objectionable in covering ourselves against all possible contingencies . . .

MRS ALVING

Nor do I.

MANDERS

. . . but what about the people round here, how would they react? That's something you know better than I.

MRS ALVING

H'm, people's reactions . . .

MANDERS

Would there be any considerable body of responsible opinion— really responsible opinion—that might take exception to it?

MRS ALVING

Well, what actually is it you mean by responsible opinion?

MANDERS

I'm thinking principally of men in independent and influential positions of the kind that makes it difficult not to attach a certain importance to their opinions.

MRS ALVING

Oh, there are plenty here of the kind that might very easily take exception if . . .

MANDERS

Well, there you are! In town we have plenty of that kind. You've only got to think of all those who support my colleague! It would be so terribly easy to interpret things as meaning that neither you nor I had a proper faith in Divine Providence.

MRS ALVING

But as far as you are concerned, my dear Pastor, you know perfectly well yourself . . .

MANDERS

Yes, I know, I know . . . my conscience is clear, that's true enough.

But all the same, we might not be able to stop people from seriously misrepresenting us. And that in turn might well have an inhibiting effect on the activities of the Orphanage.

MRS ALVING

Well, if *that* were to be the case . . .

MANDERS

Nor can I altogether disregard the difficult . . . I might well call it painful position, I might conceivably find myself in. All the influential people in town have been talking about this Orphanage. It's partly intended to benefit the town, of course, and people are hoping it will help considerably towards reducing the burden on the rates. But since I have acted as your adviser and looked after the business side of things, I rather fear the more zealous ones would turn on *me* in the first place . . .

MRS ALVING

Yes, that risk you mustn't run.

MANDERS

To say nothing of the attacks that would undoubtedly be made on me in certain papers and periodicals . . .

MRS ALVING

You've said enough, my dear Pastor Manders. That settles it.

MANDERS

So you don't want any insurance?

MRS ALVING

No, we'll let it go.

MANDERS (leaning back in his chair)

But if there did happen to be an accident? You never know . . . would you be able to make good the damage?

MRS ALVING

No, I can tell you straight, I wouldn't.

MANDERS

Well, you know, Mrs. Alving . . . this is really a grave responsibility we are taking upon ourselves.

MRS ALVING

But *can* we do anything else, do you think?

MANDERS

No, that's just it. In fact, we *can't*. We mustn't run the risk of giving people the wrong impression; and mustn't at any cost give offence to the general public.

MRS ALVING

You mustn't anyway, a clergyman.

MANDERS

And really I think we may assume that an institution of this kind will have luck on its side . . . indeed that it will enjoy a very special measure of protection.

MRS ALVING

Let us hope so, Pastor Manders.

Whatever may have been Ibsen's intention in presenting such a conversation as this, the fact that the idea of providence can give rise to this kind of ambiguity makes me ask whether the idea itself may not be based on a misreading of the way things are really.

Another example of a kind of thinking that has not been un-common is illustrated by the reaction of a Presbyterian father to his son's wartime experiences. On three occasions, shortly after being posted from one destroyer to another, the destroyer he had left was sunk. The old father interpreted this as evidence of special providential care. His son rejected this interpretation as he saw no reason why he should have been singled out for special treatment when his former companions had died. The idea of a discriminating providence of this kind was in his judgement un-acceptable.

Previous papers in this series have suggested that under the heading of the idea of providence men have at different periods been led to say a whole variety of different things about the character of God and his relation to the orders of nature and history. We have been reminded of those thinkers who have laboured to establish a doctrine of providence on the basis of observed empirical facts in the order of the physical universe. But what set anybody off on this kind of way of looking at things? Would anybody have attempted to look for empirical evidence for a doctrine of providence if the idea of providence had not been put into the human mind from another source?

Dr Ward did not in his paper lead us to the conclusion that there is anything that could properly merit the description "the biblical doctrine of providence". Nor, I imagine, did we anticipate that he would. We have become suspicious of claims that there is "a biblical doctrine" of anything whatsoever. The word "doctrine" carries the connotation of a more systematic spelling out of a concept than the biblical literature allows us to expect in the light of our knowledge of the way in which individual books were written and eventually gathered into a corpus. On the other hand there are, in both Old and New Testaments, texts, hints, insights, suggestions, reflections which point towards a belief that human history is not entirely haphazard or fortuitous, but that there is a presence, a "divinity that shapes our ends". The fact that some thinkers have been led to string these hints and reflections together into a speculation about the way things are ultimately would seem to have arisen not from empirical observation of the order of nature but from a particular way within a community of faith of interpreting things that have happened to individuals and to groups in history. Experience of "being preserved" and "brought safely through" when reflected on over a period of years in a community of faith would be likely to give rise to convictions about God's government of the universe.

John Macquarrie, whose thinking about the idea of providence has greatly influenced my own thinking as will be seen, directs attention to the story of Joseph and the story of the Exodus as two stories which have powerfully affected, and perhaps been affected by, the attitude towards ultimate reality of the Hebrew community of faith.[1] In the story of Joseph events turned out for good in spite of the malign intentions of his brothers. The conclusion drawn from this experience is: "It was not you who sent me here, but God". The story of the Exodus is even more powerfully formative of Israel's thinking about herself and about Yahweh. Whatever the plain historical happening, the story has been elaborated into a story of high theological significance. Reflection on experience has led to a theological interpretation of that experience which has in time led to embellishment of the story as told and retold within the community of faith. God is to be thought of as the kind of God who does this sort of thing for his people. Jeremiah 23. 7-8 suggests that even this Exodus paradigm of God's care for his people will give way to the story of his liberation of his people from subsequent exile in Babylon.

> Therefore, behold, the days are coming, says the Lord, when men shall no longer say, "As the Lord lives who brought up the people of Israel out of the land of Egypt", but "As the Lord lives who brought up and led the descendents of the house of Israel out of the north country where he had driven them".

This is no wishful thinking. The prophets have reached a deep conviction about the relation of Yahweh to his people, a conviction born, we must suggest, out of long reflection in the community of faith on the community's historical experience interpreted in the dimension of faith. History is seen as Yahweh's workshop: as holy and righteous he makes hard demands; as merciful he reconciles and forgives. But in it all he watches over his people, disciplining and teaching them through events and their reaction to events, so that they may be a better instrument of his historical purposes among the nations. The emphasis is not so much a favoured-nation treatment, or protection, but rather a purposive caring with an eye to the future.

Inheriting these traditional attitudes and beliefs and expectations, the friends of Jesus could hardly fail to seek an interpretation

[1] John Macquarrie, *Principles of Christian Theology* (1966), p. 221.

of the life and death of Jesus in relation to this conviction about the active historical concern of Yahweh. The paradigm of a geographical exodus was transposed into an act of liberation in the moral, psychological, spiritual, and eschatological realm. The cross and its liberating after-effect was but the latest and most potent expression of God's loving care. Already in the Gospel pericope of the Transfiguration this transposition has taken place.

> And behold, two men talked with him, Moses and Elijah, who appeared in glory and spoke of his departure [τὴν ἔξοδον αὐτοῦ] which he was to accomplish at Jerusalem. (Luke 9.30-1).

It is then arguable that a continuity of thought can be traced from an individual and group conviction that he and they have experienced the caring help of God in things that have happened to them, to a community-belief that this and that particular event is an instance and expression of God's caring rule over all history and all nature. Once a community-belief is established then new members are initiated into this belief; it becomes formative of their own attitude and approach to things that happen. Experience, reflection on experience, interpretation of experience as reflected on—these come first. But once a belief is established in a community of faith the doctrine is assimilated by the minds of new members before it is tested by experience, and the believer finds himself looking for evidence of the truth of the doctrine in his subsequent experience. The formative, attitude-conditioning influences of the doctrine of a community of faith are very powerful indeed (as for example the eschatological expectations of members of Adventist sects).

If, however, this is roughly true as an analysis of the process by which a particular way of looking at things came to be elaborated in a community of faith, it is also possible for this elaboration to be expressed in a form which is subsequently discredited by experience. If a spirit of inquiry develops within the community of faith, then the received doctrines are vulnerable, exposed to a more and more rigorous scrutiny and criticism if they seem no longer to give a satisfactory account of experience or to be too *simpliste* in formulation in the light of new knowledge of the universe. Students of those movements of thought we call the Renaissance and the Reformation can observe criticism being applied to the received doctrines of the medieval Church.

John Macquarrie illustrates this process of criticizing doctrine in the light of changing circumstances and new knowledge with reference to Calvin's doctrine of providence. He sees Calvin's doctrine as coming close to a kind of fatalism. A belief in fate accepts that whatever happens has been determined in advance by some sovereign agent; it excludes in its extreme form free will and human responsibility. In the view of the prophets men are responsible; even if their freedom and responsibility is limited by the boundaries of what is involved in being human, within these boundaries men have freedom and are accountable. Calvin in his concern to uphold the sovereignty of God debases the relationship between man and God "to the subpersonal level where man is little more than a puppet and God too has been degraded to the one who pulls the strings". Macquarrie quotes as an example of this Calvinistic tendency to say things which appear to make nonsense of any idea of human responsibility: "Men do nothing save at the secret instigation of God, and do not discuss or deliberate on anything but what he has previously decreed with himself and brings to pass by his secret directions".[2]

What point then have we reached along this line of argument? If belief in providence arises out of an interpretation of the way things have turned out for certain individuals and groups, that belief obtains within a community of faith and must constantly be checked in the light of the experience of the community in the course of the changes which make up human history. Such a checking of the theology of Calvin has led to considerable modification in the thinking even of those for whom Calvin is the theologian *par excellence*. We may therefore say in general about theological formulations that, so long as a rigorous scrutiny and criticism is maintained within the community of faith, the community will be safeguarded against the most damaging effects of mistaken or one-sided doctrines. Nevertheless, whatever modification may have been made in the emphasis of Calvin's thought, it would be hard to deny that popular ideas of providence, in so far as they still circulate in the sub-conscious minds of modern men and women, do seem to reflect a degree of distortion which makes me ask again whether a doctrine of providence can be rescued and restated. Are we honestly able to state that God works in such a way that to speak of it as "providence" is a valid way to speak of it? The idea of God as controller of the universe endowed with foreknowledge, prevision, and oversight of events, raises enormous difficulties of which the human experience of evil and suffering is by no means the least.

The *experience* of evil and suffering is a *problem* only for those who believe that behind the flux of events is a sovereign will which is both benevolent and powerful. For anyone who allows himself both to see human suffering in its distribution and

[2] Ibid., p. 224.

depth and also to believe in a traditional doctrine of God as originator of the whole process, the *problem* posed is excruciating. Some who write about this problem seem to be so concerned to protect their concept of God that they underestimate the full horror of the human predicament. If natural calamities raise questions for a doctrine of providence as it affects the ordering of the physical universe as the stage on which the human drama is to be played, the actual experienced sufferings, privations, degradations of human beings in history call in question faith's attempt to affirm a consistent ultimate purpose of love; it is, after all, the insights of Christian faith which have raised our sense of the individual worth of the human person. Some of the ways in which human beings suffer and die are obscene beyond anything that can be said in amelioration. Can a doctrine of providence fully and frankly include within its purview these revolting outrages against the human dignity which the doctrine itself implies? Christian apologists have not always allowed themselves to face the facts of life; some seem determined to believe in God and his goodness and providence no matter what happens. Could it be that our way of understanding the goodness and providence of God is at fault seeing that there is no doubt at all about the fact and wide spread of human misery? Does the act of creation itself reduce God's own freedom to alter the process once started? In the act of procreation men and women deliberately bring into existence a new life, a new being; up to a point they guard and care for this new being; but only up to a point. The child may have some inherent physical defect which will cause it to suffer in years ahead; no parents can prevent their adult children from making decisions which can cause only unhappiness for themselves and others. In some cases parents are responsible and powerless. Their attitude towards their suffering children may continue to be of the deepest caring and loving concern, but beyond being there in an attitude of love and readiness there is nothing they can do. If human beings continually take this kind of risk in begetting children, may we not by analogy say that God took a risk of a similar kind but of immeasurably greater magnitude when he brought into being and continues to sustain a universe in which obscenities and degradations can happen? When all has been said on the other side about the triumph of the human spirit over suffering and the fine flowering of human character in the encounter with frustration and pain, are we really able to hope that in the end of the day it will be possible to believe that the final result will be seen to be such that the risk of creation was justified, that the final good will justify the evil and the heart-rending pain?

It is this problem above all which makes me ask whether the hard facts of human historical experience can allow us to hold a doctrine of providence in its traditional form within the community of faith. While faith is personal commitment in trust to a view of things which cannot be empirically verified, there must surely be a point beyond which credulity cannot be stretched in the face of contradictory facts. May it not be that in rethinking what we can believe about the relation between God and our actual experience as men and women we shall have to look more deeply into that emphasis which we find in Dietrich Bonhoeffer's *Letters and Papers* in which he speaks of the helplessness of God in the world?

> He [God] is weak and powerless in the world, and that is precisely the way, the only way, in which he is with us and helps us. . . . Here is the decisive difference between Christianity and all religions. Man's religiosity makes him look in his distress to the power of God in the world : God is the *Deus ex machina*. The Bible directs man to God's powerlessness and suffering; only the suffering God can help.[3]

Can it be that as Christians we have never really faced the implications for our doctrine of God in his relation to the world of the uniquely Christian concept of a God who suffers? And what does this mean in relation to the doctrine of creation? Does it imply that God could not help himself—that being who he is it was inevitable that he should share his Being and that in letting others be he brought about a situation in which he became powerless as a human parent is sometimes powerless? Is the human tragedy inherent in the being and character of the love which is at the heart of all things? If so, can the "model" of providence with its central idea of foresight, foreknowledge, and government really be operated meaningfully in relation to a concept of God which is genuinely "re-drawn" in the light of the cross, of which Paul said : "The weakness of God is stronger than men." Is our problem once again that the God of the philosophers has never been fully Christianized?

Whatever else the phrase "the death of God" may mean, it is being used to give theological expression to changed psycho-social conditions. As Dorothea Sölle puts the matter : "It points to the experience of the end of all immediate certainty, whether objective and universal or subjective and private."[4] No modern man can say

[3] D. Bonhoeffer, *Letters and Papers from Prison* (1967 rev. trans.), pp. 196-7
[4] Dorothea Sölle, *Christ the Representative* (1967), p. 12.

with confidence: "God's in his heaven—All's right with the world." Norman Pittenger is another writer who sees the need to reconceptualize our ideas of God,[5] and, if his argument were to be held a sound argument, then inevitably that aspect of God's character and relationship with the world which the doctrine of providence was designed to express would come in for radical re-examination. It could be that a reconceptualized doctrine of creation, reconciliation, and fulfilment would eliminate the need for a separate formulation to say whatever used to be said by a doctrine of providence. John Macquarrie would seem to be moving in this direction.

He makes the point that only if creation is thought of as an event in the past does it become necessary to bring forward a distinct doctrine of providence to establish God's continuing interest in the world. The need does not arise if the doctrine of creation is taken to mean not the initial dynamic, but the "continuing dependence of the beings at all times on Being that lets them be". On the other hand, Macquarrie argues that creativity is not just random creativity, but has a positive character of which purposefulness in human activities might provide an analogy. He wishes therefore to retain the doctrine of providence as a statement of what he calls "an ordered movement into ever fuller and richer kinds of being. Faith in providence asserts this definite movement in the creation, an overcoming of deficiencies and distortions and a fuller realising of potentialities." Elsewhere he writes: "The belief in providence does assert a direction in events, a direction which we can sometimes know as grace as we move with it, sometimes as judgement when we go against it; and this direction is toward ever fuller being."[6]

I find myself helped by this Macquarrie-talk about a "direction", a kind of moral grain of the universe; move along with it and you experience it as grace; move against the grain and you experience it as judgement.

The "model" of a "direction" suggests movement and growth; it keeps open freedom to go with it or against it; it indicates that neither the way towards fulfilment is foreordained nor the end-result foreclosed; the possibility of growth and fulfilment is open. And it carries as a corollary the idea of God as one who is totally open and able to "take" whatever happens and in the omnipotence of love "cope" creatively with whatever comes. There is in other words no foreordained future; the future is made out of the happenings and reactions and choices of the present; but whatever

[5] W. Norman Pittenger, *Process Thought and Christian Faith*. 1968.
[6] Op. cit., pp. 219 and 223.

God is presented with as a result of these decisions he is able in love to handle creatively. Wounds can be changed into scars and the scars become part of the finished work. The Creator took the risk of giving freedom to beings other than himself, but, without diminishing their freedom, he is never defeated by any situation with which they confront him.

On the very important issues raised by asking what is the bearing of belief in providence on the practice of prayer I can do no more than direct attention to a recent careful discussion of these issues by Peter Baelz in his book *Prayer and Providence* (1968).

The teachings of Jesus, his own way of coping with what came to him in his particular circumstances, his death and the way he died, and what others have discovered in reaction to that teaching and that life and that death of the way in which the hazards of life can be met and lived with and lived through and assimilated— all this has become a vast storehouse in the community of faith of evidence both that there is a "direction" and that joys and sorrows alike can be so accepted and handled that the outcome is enhanced awareness and sensitivity, and the increase of personal being and value for others.

To put this another way, I would say that Christian faith and experience have led many to discover that in the exploration of life there is no situation that is incapable of being so handled that the evil in it is neutralized and absorbed and transformed into more understanding and more love. To overcome evil with good is not impossible; when this happens, there results an enhancement, an enrichment of personalness.

This, I take it, is what Paul is saying in Romans 8.28: "We know that in everything God works for good with those who love him." But Paul doesn't stop there. He goes on with all that difficult argument about "those whom he foreknew he also predestined to be conformed to the image of his Son". It is hard for us to read these words without the shadow of what Calvin made of them falling across the page. Perhaps all Paul intends is to safeguard the initiative and grace of God lest any man should think that it is in virtue of his own co-operative attitudes that things work out for good. If that is so, then Paul may primarily be saying no more and no less than that there is no situation that falls outside God's capacity for exercising a transfiguring love in the lives of those who seek God in the situation.

Is it possible, is it necessary, to go on from these spiritual discoveries of faith to make universal claims about a purposeful providential caring for the whole human and physical universe? Can we argue a universal case from some particular instances, when there are so many other particular instances where we do not see this happening: situations in which evil breeds evil, in which suffering brutalizes and corrupts; situations in which people have never learned that there is a Presence of such loving power that the evil in their circumstances can be transformed into its opposite? I think that we can only argue a universal case if it includes that insight which Bonhoeffer calls "the helplessness of God in the world". If God is not in some sense helpless, how can he be held to be good in face of the sufferings of men? Even if we acknowledge that view of the way things are which Macquarrie has called a "direction", we are still left baffled by the apparent failure of so many to find that help in their sufferings which belief in the existence of this "direction" would bring to them.

When I ask myself in the midst of all my questionings and perplexities what I really believe, I find I must say that I believe in a presence and power of love which is indestructible because all that evil can do to this love is to give it ever fresh opportunities of loving. I believe in this presence and power of love because this is supremely what I have seen in Jesus crucified, and what I have seen in the lives of certain other people, and what I have discovered to be true in my own experience not so much by achieving this love as by failing to achieve it and yet knowing it to be achievable and real. I believe in this presence and power of love and I want to try to live my life this way because, of all the possible ways of living human life, this seems to be the only way that is self-authenticating, self-evidently true. I believe too, though I do not know how to formulate this, that in this presence and power of love lies the meaning of the mysterious experience of humanity and history in which we are all involved. I believe that the reality of which I have been speaking is a glimpse of the reality that Christians traditionally point towards when they use the word God.

This is a faith to live by. But I find it very difficult to spell out the universal implications of this in the direction of a doctrine of the relation between God and the world of men which does not raise as many difficulties as it resolves. I have tried to point in a direction I believe to be true—but I am very tentative about suggesting that it points towards a Christian doctrine of providence.